CAMBRIDGE LIBRARY COLLECTION

Books of enduring scholarly value

Perspectives from the Royal Asiatic Society

A long-standing European fascination with Asia, from the Middle East to China and Japan, came more sharply into focus during the early modern period, as voyages of exploration gave rise to commercial enterprises such as the East India companies, and their attendant colonial activities. This series is a collaborative venture between the Cambridge Library Collection and the Royal Asiatic Society of Great Britain and Ireland, founded in 1823. The series reissues works from the Royal Asiatic Society's extensive library of rare books and sponsored publications that shed light on eighteenth- and nineteenth-century European responses to the cultures of the Middle East and Asia. The selection covers Asian languages, literature, religions, philosophy, historiography, law, mathematics and science, as studied and translated by Europeans and presented for Western readers.

A Grammar of the Bengal Language

The language of Bangladesh, West Bengal and parts of Tripura and Assam, Bengali is an Indo-Aryan language originating from Sanskrit. With over 230 million speakers, it is the sixth most spoken language in the world today. Published in 1778, this was one of the first grammars of Bengali ever compiled. The English orientalist Nathaniel Brassey Halhed (1751–1830) prepared the work during his employment with the East India Company, in order to facilitate communication between his colleagues and the weaving districts of Bengal. It provides detailed and descriptive accounts of all aspects of the language, from its alphabet to its systems of agreement, case and tense, as well as its numerals, verbs and word order. The work was considered to be groundbreaking because Halhed made the first steps towards identifying the Indo-European language family, making it of lasting relevance to language typologists today.

Cambridge University Press has long been a pioneer in the reissuing of out-of-print titles from its own backlist, producing digital reprints of books that are still sought after by scholars and students but could not be reprinted economically using traditional technology. The Cambridge Library Collection extends this activity to a wider range of books which are still of importance to researchers and professionals, either for the source material they contain, or as landmarks in the history of their academic discipline.

Drawing from the world-renowned collections in the Cambridge University Library and other partner libraries, and guided by the advice of experts in each subject area, Cambridge University Press is using state-of-the-art scanning machines in its own Printing House to capture the content of each book selected for inclusion. The files are processed to give a consistently clear, crisp image, and the books finished to the high quality standard for which the Press is recognised around the world. The latest print-on-demand technology ensures that the books will remain available indefinitely, and that orders for single or multiple copies can quickly be supplied.

The Cambridge Library Collection brings back to life books of enduring scholarly value (including out-of-copyright works originally issued by other publishers) across a wide range of disciplines in the humanities and social sciences and in science and technology.

A Grammar of the Bengal Language

Nathaniel Brassey Halhed

CAMBRIDGE UNIVERSITY PRESS

Cambridge, New York, Melbourne, Madrid, Cape Town,
Singapore, São Paolo, Delhi, Mexico City

Published in the United States of America by Cambridge University Press, New York

www.cambridge.org
Information on this title: www.cambridge.org/9781108056359

© in this compilation Cambridge University Press 2013

This edition first published 1778
This digitally printed version 2013

ISBN 978-1-108-05635-9 Paperback

বোধপ্রকাশৎ শব্দশাস্ত্রৎ
ফিরিঙ্গিনামুপকারার্থৎ
ক্রিয়তে হালেদদ্ধেঞ্জী

A
GRAMMAR
OF THE
BENGAL LANGUAGE

BY

NATHANIEL BRASSEY HALHED.

ইন্দুদায়োপি যস্যান্তৎ নয়যুঃ শব্দবারিধেঃ।
পুক্রিয়ান্তস্য কৃৎস্নস্য ক্ষমোবক্তু নরঃ কথৎ॥

PRINTED

AT

HOOGLY IN BENGAL

M DCC LXXVIII.

PREFACE.

THE wisdom of the Britiſh Parliament has within theſe few years taken a deciſive part in the internal policy and civil adminiſtration of its Aſiatic territories ; and more particularly in the Kingdom of Bengal, which, by the moſt formal act of authority in the eſtabliſhment of a Supreme Court of Juſtice, it has profeſſedly incorporated with the Britiſh Empire. Much however ſtill remains for the completion of this grand work ;

and

and we may reafonably prefume, that one of its moft important defiderata is the cultivation of a right underftanding and of a general medium of intercourfe between the Government and its Subjects ; between the Natives of Europe who are to rule, and the Inhabitants of India who are to obey.   The Romans, a people of little learning and lefs tafte, had no fooner conquered Greece than they applied themfelves to the ftudy of Greek : They adopted its Laws even before they could read them, and civilized themfelves in fubduing their enemies.   The Englifh, who have made fo capital a progrefs in the Polite Arts, and who are mafters of Bengal, may, with more eafe and greater propriety, add its Language to their acquifitions : that they may explain the benevolent principles of that legiflation whofe decrees they inforce ; that they may convince while they command; and be at once the difpenfers of Laws and of Science to an extenfive nation.   This fubject has hitherto been utterly difregarded in Europe ; and it is fcarcely believed that Bengal ever poffeffed a native and peculiar dialect of its own, diftinct from that idiom which, under the name of *Moor's*, has been fuppofed to prevail over all India.   To remove thefe prejudices, and to contribute my flender mite to the public fervice, I have attempted the following grammatical explanation of the vernacular language of

Bengal

Bengal : in which my principal aim has been to comprehend every thing neceffary to be known ; not contenting myfelf with a fuperficial or partial view, nor confining mv obfervations to the more obvious particularities. A fhort treatife, when preceded by other more copious and diffufive compilations on the fame fubject, may perhaps pafs for a judicious àbftract, or an elegant compendium ; but every omiffion of the writer who hath cho-fen an unhandled topic will be imputed to ignorance or neglect, by thofe whofe fubfequent difcoveries may have furnifhed more complete information.

The grand Source of Indian Literature, the Parent of almoft every dialect from the Perfian Gulph to the China Seas, is the Shanfcrit ; a language of the moft venerable and unfathomable antiquity ; which although at prefent fhut up in the libraries of Bramins, and appropriated folely to the records of their Religi-on, appears to have been current over moft of the Oriental World ; and traces of its original extent may ftill be difcovered in almoft every diftrict of Afia. I have been aftonifhed to find the fimilitude of Shanfcrit words with thofe of Perfian and Ara-bic, and even of Latin and Greek : and thefe not in technical and metaphorical terms, which the mutuation of refined arts and improved manners might have occafionally inntroduced ; but

in

in the main ground-work of language, in monofyllables, in the
the names of numbers, and the appellations of fuch things as
would be firft difcriminated on the immediate dawn of civiliza-
tion. The refemblance which may be obferved in the characters upon the medals and fignets of various diftricts of Afia, the
light which they reciprocally reflect upon each other, and the
general analogy which they all bear to the fame grand Prototype, afford another ample field for curiofity. The coins of
Affam, Napaul, Cafhmeere and many other kingdoms are all
ftamped with Shanfcrit letters, and moftly contain allufions to
the old Shanfcrit Mythology : the fame conformity I have obferved on the impreffions of feals from Bootan and Tibet. A
collateral inference may likewife be deduced from the pecul ar
arrangement of the Shanfcrit alphabet, fo very different from
that of any other quarter of the world. This extraordinary
mode of combination ftill exifts in the greateft part of the Eaft,
from the Indus to Pegu, in dialects now apparently unconnected,
and in characters compleatly diffimilar ; but is a forcible argument that they are all derived from the fame fource. Another
channel of fpeculation prefents itfelf in the names of perfons and
places, of titles and dignities, which are open to general notice,
and in which, to the fartheft limits of Afia, may be found ma-

nifeft

manifeſt traces of the Shanſcrit. The meagre remnants of Coptic antiquities afford no ſcope for compariſon between that idiom and this primitive tongue: but there ſtill exiſts ſufficient grounds for conjecture that Egypt has but a diſputable claim to its long-boaſted originality in language, in policy and in religion. In ſupport of this opinion I ſhall mention only one circumſtance. The Raja of Kiſhenagur, who is by much the moſt learned and able antiquary which Bengal has produced within this century, has very lately affirmed, that he has in his own poſſeſſion Shanſcrit books which give an account of a communication formerly ſubſiſting between India and Egypt; wherein the Egyptians are conſtantly deſcribed as diſciples, not as inſtructors, and as ſeeking that liberal education and thoſe ſciences in Hindoſtan, which none of their own countrymen had ſufficient knowledge to impart. The few paſſages which are extant in the antient Greek authors reſpecting the Bracmans at the ſame time that they receive a freſh light from this relation, very ſtrongly corroborate its authenticity.

But though theſe ſeveral proofs of the former prevalence of the Shanſcrit are now thinly ſcattered over an immenſe continent, and interſperſed with an infinite variety of extraneous matter, arriſing from every poſſible revolution in the manners

and

and principles of the nations, who have by turns cultivated or destroyed it; that part of Asia between the Indus and the Ganges still preserves the whole language pure and inviolate; still offers a thousand books to the perusal of the curious, many of which have been religiously handed down from the earliest periods of human existance.

The Jesuit Dupont has misled many subsequent writers, by his fabulous account of the wonderful structure of this dialect. According to him, it owes the most extensive and copious harvest of words to a very inadequate number of primitive roots, and these he chuses to call the *caput mortuum* of the language; as not being words of themselves, but certain sounds bearing a relation to certain ideas. The elements to which he alludes, and of which he has misquoted an instance, fall far short of those comprehensive faculties which he has bestowed on them. They are simply the Roots of Verbs, and are even so denominated in the very title of the book from whence he must have borrowed his inaccurate examples. Their number is about seven hundred; and it must be granted that to them, as to the verbs of most other languages, a very plentiful stock of verbal nouns owes its origin; but I by no means believe that they exceed those of the Greek either in quantity or variety.

The

The fundamental part of the Shanfcrit language is divided into three claffes: *Dhaat* or roots of verbs, (Dupont's primitive elements) *Shubd* or original nouns, and *Evya* or particles. Thefe latter are ever indeclinable as in other idioms : but the words comprehended in the two former claffes muft be prepared by certain additions and inflexions to fit them for a place in compofition. And here it is that the art of the Grammarian has found room to expand itfelf, and to employ all the powers of refinement. Not a fyllable, not a letter can be added or altered but by regimen ; not the moft trifling variation of the fenfe in the minuteft fubdivifion of declenfion or conjugation can be effected without the application of feveral rules : and all the different forms for every change of gender, number, cafe, perfon, tenfe, mood or degree are methodically arranged for the affiftance of the memory; refembling (though on a fcale infinitely more extenfive) the compilations of *propria quae maribus* and *as in prefenti.*

Had Dupont been lefs bigotted to his fyftem of a *caput mortuum*, he muft have reflected that a verb and a noun are equally neceffary to the conftruction of a fentence, and to the very intelligibility of fpeech; and had he gained a proper infight into the Shanfcrit, he would have been fully convinced, that its elementary parts are made up of thefe two genera with the addition of particles.

b

To

To this triple fource I conceive that every word of truly Indian original in every provincial and fubordinate dialect of all Hindoftan may ftill be traced by a laborious and critical analyfis; and all fuch terms as are thoroughly proved to bear no relation to any one of the Shanfcrit roots, I would confider as the production of fome remote and foreign idiom, fubfequently ingrafted upon the main ftock. A judicious inveftigation of this principle would probably throw a new light upon the firft invention of many arts and fciences, and open a frefh mine of philological difcoveries.

Exclufive of the Shanfcrit, there are three different dialects applied (tho' not with equal currency) in the kingdom of Bengal : Viz. the Perfian, the Hindoftanic and the proper Bengalefe ; each of which has its own peculiar department in the bufinefs of the country, and confequently neither of them can be univerfally adopted to the exclufion of the others.

The Perfian entered Bengal with the Mogul conquerors, and being the language of the court naturally gained a footing in the law and in the revenues ; it has alfo for fome centuries been the common medium of negotiation between the feveral ftates of Hindoftan, and from thence became an almoft indifpenfable qualification for thofe who were to manage the extenfive affairs of

the

the Eaſt India Company : ſo that the accurate and elegant grammar compoſed by Mr. Jones does equal honour to the cauſe of learning, and ſervice to his countrymen in Aſia. This language is ſtill uſed by all the Mogul officers of government, in their ſeveral departments of accounts and correſpondence; as being the dialect of the former ruling power, of which the Engliſh have in ſome degree taken the place, and whoſe ſyſtem they have not yet laid aſide. From hence ariſes one capital impediment to the uniformity of political arrangements in Bengal; for while the ſummary of all public buſineſs is kept in one idiom, the detail is invariably confined to another, as I ſhall preſently demonſtrate.

The Hindoſtanic, or Indian language, appears to have been generally ſpoken for many ages through all proper Hindoſtan. It is indubitably derived from the Shanſcrit, with which it has exactly the ſame connexion, as the modern dialects of France and Italy with pure Latin. For while the ſame ſounds are almoſt conſtantly applied in both languages to repreſent the ſame ideas, the inflexions by which they are affected and the modes of grammatical regimen are widely different. The Shanſcrit has a dual number both to verbs and nouns, the Hindoſtanic to neither. Verbs in Shanſcrit have the ſame form for

both

both the mafculine and feminine genders ; Hindoftanic verbs are diftinguifhed by different terminations for the different fexes, like thofe of the Arabic. Thefe are their capital outlines of diffimilarity ; but in the original appropriation of particular words to particular fenfes, in the idiomatic turns of expreffion and complexion of fpeech we may obferve the ftrongeft family likenefs.

The Charaċters alfo peculiar to the Hindoftanic are exaċtly the fame with thofe of the Shanfcrit, but of a ruder fhape : yet ftill .exhibiting a more accurate refemblance than is found in many of the Greek letters upon infcriptions of different Æras.

This primitive Hindoftanic tongue has by no means preferved its purity, or its univerfality to the prefent age : for the modern Inhabitants of India vary almoft as much in language as in Religion. It is well known in what an obftinate and inviolable obfcurity the Jentoos conceal as well the Myfteries of their Faith, as the Books in which they are contained : and under what fevere prohibitions their moft approved Legiflators have confined the ftudy of the Shanfcrit to their own principal tribes only. An explanation of it to perfons not qualified for this fcience by their rank, fubjeċted both the teacher and the pupil to very tremendous penalties ; but to fully its purity by imparting the flighteft knowledge of it to ftrangers was ever cautioufly avoided as the moft inexpiable crime. The Pundit who imparted a fmall

portion

portion of his language to me, has by no means efcaped the cenfure of his countrymen : and while he readily difplayed the principles of his grammar, he has invariably refufed to develope a fingle article of his religion. Thus we may fuppofe that when the Mahometan Invaders firft fettled in India, and from the neceffity of having fome medium of communication with their new fubjects, applied themfelves to the ftudy of the Hindoftanic dialect, the impenetrable referve of the Jentoos would quickly render its abftrufer Shanfcrit terms unintelligible ; and the Foreigners, unpracticed in the idiom, would frequently recur to their own native expreffions. New adventurers continually arriving kept up a conftant influx of exotic words, and the heterogeneous mafs gradually increafed its ftock, as conqueft or policy extended the boundaries of its circulation. But thefe alterations affected words only. The grammatical principles of the original Hindoftanic, and the ancient forms of conjugation and inflexion remained the fame ; and whilft the primitive fubftantives were excluded or exchanged, the verbs maintained both their inflexions and their regimen. They ftill fubfift in their priftine ftate ; and at prefent thofe perfons are thought to fpeak this compound idiom with the moft elegance, who mix with pure Indian verbs the greateft number of Perfian and Arabic nouns. Such of the Hindoos as have been connected with the Muffel-

man

man courts, or admitted to any offices under that government have generally complimented their masters by a compliance with these literary innovations. But the Bramins and all other well-educated Jentoos, whose ambition has not overpowered their principles, still adhere with a certain conscientious tenacity to their primeval tongue, and have many antient books written in its purest style ; among which were probably the celebrated Fables of Pilpay (now not to be found.) They continue to apply it to the purposes of commerce in Surat, Guzarat and other places on the western Coast ; and their correspondence circulates through all Hindoftan, quite to the interior parts of Bengal ; where several Bankers of this Religion, who have at different times emigrated from the higher countries, carry on a very extensive traffic. The Characters in which it is written, though all derived from the Shanscrit, deviate as much from their original exemplar, as our running-hand and italian differ from round-hand. It is said that there are seven different forts of Indian hands all comprized under the general term *Naagoree*, which may be interpreted *Writing* ; and the elegant Shanscrit is styled *Daeb Naogoree* or the *Writing of the Immortals* ; which may not improbably be a refinement from the more simple and unpolished Naagoree of the earlier ages. The word *Taugoree* is sometimes

times ufed to fignify a loofe or inaccurate character of the Naagoree, but I never could difcover that any precife diftinction
was implied by it. The Bengal letters, fuch as difplayed in the
following fheets, are another branch of the fame ftock; lefs
beautiful than the refined Shanfcrit, but refembling it no lefs
than the Naagoree. They are ufed in *Affam* as well as in Bengal, and may be probably one of the moft antient modes of writing in the world. The Bengalefe Bramins have all their Shanfcrit books copied in this national alphabet, and tranfpofe into it
all the *Daeb Naagoree* manufcripts for their own perufal.

The dialect called by us the *Moors* is that mixed fpecies of
Hindoftanic, which I have above defcribed to owe its exiftance
to the Mahometan Conquefts. In this idiom feveral elegant
poems and tales have been compofed by learned Perfian and
Mogul authors, and are ftill extant in the libraries of the curious.
Thefe are always written in the Perfian hand, which is by no
means calculated for expreffing the found either of the Hindoftanic vowels or nafal confonants. The Mahometans of the lower rank have a few books on Religious fubjects in this language, and in the Naagoree characters; which are alfo ufed by
fome of them in their petty accounts. Europeans on their arrival in India, reduced to a neceffary intercourfe with Mahome-

tan

tan fervants, or Sepoys, habitually acquire from them this idiom in that imperfect and confined ftate which is the confequence of the menial condition of their inftructors : yet this curious fyftem of ftudy hath produced more than one attempt to a Grammar and Vocabulary. The jargon however, fuch as it is, proves utterly unintelligible to the villagers and peafants both in Hindoftan and Bengal, nor is ufed any where, but in large towns frequented by Mahometans and Strangers. On this dialect an ingenious Miffionary long fince publifhed a laborious treatife in Latin. He is the earlieft and may be deemed the only writer on the fubject, for the latter compofitions do not deferve a name.

What the pure Hindoftanic is to upper India, the language which I have here endeavoured to explain is to Bengal, intimately related to the Shanfcrit both in expreffions, conftruction and character. It is the fole channel of perfonal and epiftolary communication among the Hindoos of every occupation and tribe. All their bufinefs is tranfacted, and all their accounts are kept in it; and as their fyftem of education is in general very confined, there are few among them who can write or read any other idiom : the uneducated, or eight parts in ten of the whole nation, are neceffarily confined to the ufage of their mother tongue.

The

The Board of Commerce at Calcutta, and the feveral Chiefs of the fubordinate Factories cannot properly conduct the India Company's mercantile correfpondence and negotiations, without the intermediate agency of Bengal Interpre ers: for the whole fyftem of the Inveftment, in every ftage of its preparation and provifion, is managed in the language of the country; in which all the accounts of the Aurungs, (or manufacturing towns) thofe of the Company's Export Warehoufe all propofals and letters from agents, merchants, contractors, weavers, -winders, bleachers &c. are conftantly prefented; and into which all orders to Gomaftahs, Aumeens and other officers for the purchafe and procuration of goods muft be tranflated.

Important as this language muft confequently appear to the Commercial line, its adoption would be no lefs beneficial to the Revenue department. For although the Contracts, Leafes and other obligations, executed between Government and its immediate dependants and tenants, continue to be drawn out in the Perfian dialect, yet the under Leafes and engagements, which thefe in their turn grant to the peafants and cultivators of the ground, and all thofe copyhold tenures called *Pottahs* are conftantly written in Bengalefe. And it may even be doubted whether more than one third of all Jentoo Zemindars, Farmers and other Leffees of the ftate can read a fingle word of their

own accounts and reprefentations, as delivered in their Moon-
fhee's Perfian tranflation.

The internal policy of the kingdom demands an equal fhare
of attention ; and the many impofitions to which the poorer clafs
of people are expofed, in a country ftill fluctuating between the
relics of former defpotic dominion, and the liberal fpirit of its
prefent legiflature, have long cried out for a remedy. This has
lately been propofed in the appointment of gentlemen of mature
experience in the manners and cuftoms of the natives to the fe-
véral divifions and diftricts of Bengal, to act as jufticiary arbi-
trators between the head farmer and his under tenants : with
whom the indigent villager might find immediate and effectual
redrefs from the exactions of an imperious Landlord or grafp-
ing Collector, freed from the neceffary delays of an ordinary
court of juftice, and the expence and inconvenience of a regular
fuit. Such a meafure, by holding out to each induftrious indivi-
dual a near profpect of property in his earnings and feeurity in
his poffeffions, promifes, in the moft effectual manner, to enfure
ftability to our conquefts and popularity to our adminiftration ;
and will probably fet open the Britifh territories as an afylum
for the difcouraged hufbandman, the neglected artift, and op-
preffed labourer from every quarter of Hindoftan. But this
important commiffion will be more immediately, and more

exten-

extenfively beneficial, in proportion as it is conferred on
thofe only whom a competent knowledge of the Bengalefe has
previoufly qualified for a perfonal inveftigation of every unwarrantable exaction, and fcrutiny into every complicated account.

Add to this, that there is not one office under the *Nazim* or
Mogul adminiftration, nor one provincial or fubordinate court
of juftice in the kingdom where an interpreter for this language
is not judged as neceffary and as conftantly employed as for the
Perfian : and if any public notices are to be difperfed through
the country, or affixed in the great towns, they are always attended with a Bengal tranflation. In fhort, if vigour, impartia-
lity and difpatch be required to the operations of government,
to the diftribution of juftice, to the collections of the revenues
and to the tranfactions of commerce, they are only to be fecu-
red by a proper attention to that dialect ufed by the body of the
people ; efpecially as it is much better calculated both for public and private affairs by its plainnefs, its precifion and regularity of conftruction, than the flowery fentences and modulated
periods of the Perfian.

Another fingular advantage which it poffeffes, is its aptitude
for the bufinefs of the compting-houfe. For the Bengal doctrine of numbers, both in the forms of the figures and in their
application, nearly approaches to the fyftem adopted in Europe ;
from

from which nothing can more effentially differ than the Perfian mode of cyphering, both in arrangement and application : fo that thofe who would be acquainted with the latter, have a new arithmetic as well as a new language to acquire; and if they have any concerns tranfacted through this medium, they muft undergo the fubfequent trouble of reducing their Perfian accounts to the European form; whereas thofe of the Bengal accompt-ant require nothing more than an accurate copyift.

The great number of letters in the Bengal alphabet, and the intricate variety of their combinations may perhaps at firft fight ftrike the learner as an almoft infuperable difficulty. But this is his only impediment; for the grammatical part is fimple, tho' diffufe, and compleat without being complex. Its rules are plain, and its anomalies few. So that if he will refolve to gain a thorough knowledge of each particular article as he proceeds, without trifling away his time in anticipated perufals, and need-lefs references to the more advanced chapters, he will foon have reafon to be furprifed at the rapidity of his paffage over fo dif-heartening an obftacle.

Nothing need here be remarked on any particular method of ftudy; that topic has employed much abler pens. Suffice it to mention, that I have felected for this grammar as clear a fet of rules, and given it as comprehenfive an arrangement as I could devife.

devife. The tafk was rendered very laborious by the great multiplicity of obfervations I had collected, and by the frefh matter which continually occurred from my repeated applications to the Shanfcrit; of which language I have thought necef-fary to include within my defign fuch of the grammatical principles, as might throw a direct, or even a collateral light on thofe of the Bengalefe. To the curious and intelligent this will probably be the moft interefting part of the work; and I was willing to omit nothing that might tend to inftruct or to convince. For this reafon I have been fcrupuloufly minute in the infertion of examples to every rule, and prolix in my obfervations upon general grammar. The path which I have attempted to clear was never before trodden; it was neceffary that I fhould make my own choice of the courfe to be purfued, and of the land-marks to be fet up for the guidance of future travellers. I wifh-ed to obviate the recurrence of fuch erroneous opinions as may have been formed by the few Europeans who have hitherto ftu-died the Bengalefe; none of them have traced its connexion with the Shanfcrit, and therefore I conclude their fyftems muft be imperfect. For if the Arabic language (as Mr. Jones has excellently obferved) be fo intimately blended with the Perfian as to render it impoffible for the one to be accurately underftood without a moderate knowledge of the other; with ftill more pro-

priety

priety may we urge the impoffibility of learning the Bengal dia-lect without a general and comprehenfive idea of the Shanfcrit: as the union of thefe two languages is more clofe and more ge-neral; and as they bear an original relation and confanguinity to each other, which cannot even be furmifed with refpect to the Arabic and Perfian.

When the learner has made fome profiiency in the firft ru-diments, he cannot follow a more able or more expeditious guide than Mr. Jones: who in the preface to his Perfian Grammar has prefcribed an admirable fyftem of ftudy, the utility of which is abundantly proved by the wonderful extent of his own attain-ments. By an adherence to his plan this language may foon be acquired fo far as to open the way to converfation and fhort cor-refpondence with the natives; after which the progrefs of know-ledge will ever be proportionate to the affiduity of the ftu-dent.

It may not be fuperfluous in this place to remark, that a gram-mar of the pure Bengal dialect cannot be expected to convey a thorough idea of the modern jargon of the kingdom. The many political revolutions it has fuftained, have greatly im-paired the fimplicity of its language; and a long communi-cation with men of different Religions, countries and manners has rendered foreign words in fome degree familiar to a Bengal ear.

ear. The Mahometans have for the moſt part introduced ſuch terms as relate to the funćtions of their own Religion, or the excercife of their own laws and government; the Portuguefe have fupplied them with appellations of fome European arts and inventions: and in the environs of each foreign colony the idiom of the native Bengalefe is tinćtured with that of the ſtrangers who have fettled there.

Upon the fame principle, fince the influence of the Britifh nation has fuperfeded that of its former conquerors, many terms of Britifh derivation have been naturalized into the Bengal vocabulary. For as the laws, the revenues and the commerce are gradually falling into new hands and are condućted by a new fyſtem, new denominations will neceffarily arife to the excluſion of the old. The force of this obfervation may particularly be proved from thofe places in which the greateſt part of the India Company's inveſtment is provided; where a great number of the terms relating to trade are direćtly borrowed from the Englifh. So in all the country Courts of Juſtice the words *Decree, Appeal, Warrant, Summons,* and many others are conſtantly applied and underſtood by the whole body of the people.

The following work prefents the Bengal language meerly as derived from its parent the Shanfcrit. In the courfe of my defign I have avoided, with fome care, the admiſſion of ſuch

words

words as are not natives of the country, and for that reason have selected all my instances from the most authentic and antient compositions. But I would advise every person who is desirous to distinguish himself as an accurate translator to pay some attention both to the Persian and Hindostanic dialects; since in the occurrences of modern business, as managed by the present illiterate generation, he will find all his letters, representations and accounts interspersed with a variety of borrowed phrazes or unauthorized expressions. Such I hope have no place in these sheets; and as I cannot be accused of interfering with the province of those who may have illustrated either of the other dialects of India, so I may with confidence affirm that I have not been guided or assisted in my researches by those of any preceding Author. The errors and defects of this compilation are entirely my own; however copious they may be found, I have employed the most unwearied application to correct and expunge them: and if I have been in the smallest degree instrumental in attracting the attention of the curious, or in gratifying the taste of the discerning, I hope so much will be allowed me in the opposite scale.

The public curiosity must be strongly excited by the beautiful characters which are displayed in the following work: and although my attempt may be deemed incompleat or unworthy of

notice,

notice, the book itſelf will always bear an intrinſic value, from its containing as extraordinary an inſtance of mechanic abilities as has perhaps ever appeared. That the Bengal letter is very difficult to be imitated in ſteel will readily be allowed by every perſon who ſhall examine the intricacies of the ſtrokes, the unequal length and ſize of the charaĉters, and the variety of their poſitions and combinations. It was no eaſy taſk to procure a writer accurate enough to prepare an alphabet of a ſimilar and proportionate body throughout, and with that ſymmetrical exaĉtneſs which is neceſſary to the regularity and neatneſs of a fount. Mr. Bolts (who is ſuppoſed to be well verſed in this language) attempted to fabricate a ſet of types for it, with the aſſiſtance of the ableſt artiſts in London. But as he has egregiouſly failed in executing even the eaſieſt part, or primary alphabet, of which he has publiſhed a ſpecimen, there is no reaſon to ſuppoſe that his projeĉt when compleated, would have advanced beyond the uſual ſtate of imperfeĉtion to which new inventions are conſtantly expoſed.

The advice and even ſollicitation of the Governor General prevailed upon Mr. Wilkins, a gentleman who has been ſome years in the India Company's civil ſervice in Bengal, to undertake a ſet of Bengal types. He did, and his ſucceſs has exceeded every expeĉtation. In a country ſo remote from all connexion with

d

European

European artifts, he has been obliged to charge himfelf with all the various occupations of the Metallurgift the Engraver, the Founder and the Printer. To the merit of invention he was compelled to add the application of perfonal labour. With a rapidity unknown in Europe, he furmounted all the obftacles which neceffarily clog the firft rudiments of a difficult art, as well as the difadvantages of folitary experiment; and has thus fingly on the firft effort exhibited his work in a ftate of perfection which in every part of the world has appeared to require the united improvements of different projectors, and the gradual polifh of fucceffive ages.

The gentlemen at the head of Indian affairs do not want to be told of the various impofitions and forgeries with which Bengal at prefent abounds, in Pottahs, (or Leafes) in Bonds and other written fecurities of property; in Rowanahs and Duftucks, in Orders and Notices of government iffued in the country languages; as well as in all the tranfactions of commerce: and alfo in the Proceffes, Warrants and Decrees of the fupreme and inferior Courts of Judicature; all of which afford ample fcope for the exertion of Mr. Wilkins's ingenuity.

His fuccefs in this branch has enabled Great Britain to introduce all the more folid advantages of European literature among a people whom fhe has already refcued from Afiatic flavery,

very : to promote the circulation of wealth, by giving new vigour and difpatch to bufinefs, and to forward the progrefs of civil fociety by facilitating the means of intercourfe.

Even the credit of the nation is interefted in marking the progrefs of her conquefts by a liberal communication of Arts and Sciences, rather than by the effufion of blood : and policy requires that her new fubjects fhould as well feel the benefits, as the neceffity of fubmiffion.

ⓧⓧⓧⓧⓧⓧⓧⓧⓧⓧⓧ

ERRATA.

ᔓ*ʔʔʔʔʔʔʔʔʔʔʔʔ*ᔕ

Many of the errors which are here pointed out, have been revifed in the prefs, before the whole impreffion was worked off. Such of them as may yet remain, the reader is defired to correct.

Errata in the Preface.

Page iv *line* 9 *for* Cafhmeere   *read*   Cafhmeer.

    v — laft — arrifing   —   arifing.

  xxi — 9 — fuperceded   —   fuperfeded.

xxii — 11 — illuftraed   —   illuftrated.

    — 21 — excited   —   attracted.

Errata in the Grammar.

   3 — 9 — anamalous   —   anomalous.

  10 — 7 — Chaamroo   —   Chaamroo.

   — 12 — indifferetly   —   indifferently.

   — 15 — f,haaleeaa   —   f,haaleeyaa.

  19 — 4 — fhowinyo   —   fo-inyo.

  28 — 19 — রনঃ   —   নরঃ

  30 — 19 — দুতীয়া   —   দুইতীয়া

  33 — 20   the figure ক্রু *roo* ftanding for রু or r, with the fhort *oo*, is omitted by miftake.

  36 — 14 — Thucydides   —   Pherecydes.

  39 — 1 — কেন া   —   কেন

xxviii

Page 48 *line* 17 *for* হরিন *read* হরিনা

69 — 18 — রথি — রথী

78 — 12 & 13 muſt be tranſpoſed for lines 11 & 12, as the example relates to the uſage of the 6th caſe of the Shanſcrit pronoun মম *my* or *mine*.

84 — 12 after *other* inſert *rule*.

88 — 1 *for* third ſead ſecond.

109 — 10 — শুক্রবীর — শুক্রবের the poſ-[ſeſſive caſe of শুক্র

123 — 1 — করয়েজি জ্ঞাস।। — করয়ে জিজ্ঞাস।।

143 — 4 — Maahaa — Mohaa.

146 — 14 — শ্রীমন — শ্রীমান

147 — 9 inſtead of the word there uſed, ſupply রাজি *a ſinging man,* রাজী *a ſinging woman.*

Eraſe the lines 11, 12, 13 & 14. The example therein quoted is inſerted by miſtake: it relates to another article and is applied elſewhere.

line 16 *for* aſſume *read* aſſume.

— 18 — ঘুমবু — ঘুমবু and the [ſame in two places in the 20th line.

Page

Page 148 *line* 6 *for* ভাগ্যমব   *read* ভাগ্যমন্ত

   177 — 1 —   Put   — But.

   192 — 6 —   third   — ſecond.

As the letters জ and য্—শ and স are convertible in Bengaleſe, the reader·muſt not be ſurpriſed that I have uſed either of them in the ſame word indiſcriminately : A knowledge of their true application belongs only to the Shanſcrit, and will be of no uſe whatever in reading the popular dialect of Bengal.

ADDITIONS.

Page the 10th   line the laſt ———   When two vowels come together, of which the latter is ই the letter য় is ſometimes inſerted between them, with only a very ſlight naſal utterance; as তুয়ি for তুই   গোসায়ি for গোসাই &c. pronounced *too-ee* and *goſaa-ee* in both modes of ſpelling.

Page 121ſt   at the top ——   Sometimes verbs which have এ or ও in the firſt ſyllable of their infinitive, change them into ই and উ in their inflected ſtate;   as মেষন *to mix,* আমি মিষি   তোনন *to weigh,* আমি তুনি &c.

ADVERTISEMENT.

It is recommended not to bind this book till the ſetting in of the dry ſeaſon, as the greateſt part has been printed during the rains.

The Bookbinder is deſired to place the plate facing page 209.

A GRAMMAR

A
GRAMMAR

OF THE

BENGAL LANGUAGE.

CHAPTER I.

OF THE ELEMENTS.

IT is a general, but erroneous obfervation, that oriental languages are written and read from the right hand to the left;
whereas all the languages moft truly oriental, or fuch as properly belong to the whole continent of India, proceed from left to

right

right like thofe of Europe. The Arabic and the Perfian are the grand fources from whence the contrary method has been derived; and with thefe the very numerous original dialects of Hindoftan have not the fmalleft connection or refemblance.

The Natives of Bengal write with a certain flender and tough reed, very common in all the Eaft; which they fhape almoft like an European pen. They write with the hand clofed, in which they hold the pen, as the Chinefe do their writing pencil, prefsing it againft the ball of the thumb with the tip of the middle finger. The nib or point of the pen is turned downwards towards the wrift; while the thumb pointing upwards, and lying on the pen with its whole length keeps it firm againft the middle joint of the fore finger.

As they have neither chairs nor tables, their pofture in writing is very different from ours: They fit upon their heels, or fometimes upon their hams, while their left hand held open ferves as a defk whereon to lay the paper on which they write, which is kept in its place by the thumb: fo that they never write on a large fheet of paper without folding it down to a very fmall furface.

The

The great number of letters, the complex mode of combination, and the difficulty of pronunciation are confiderable impediments to the ftudy of the Bengal language; and the careleffnefs and ignorance of the people have much aggravated the inconvenience by the univerfal inaccuracy of their writings: Into which they introduce fo many anamalous characters, and fo frequently deviate from the original forms, that they feldom can read each others hand-writing without hefitation and interruption. Many of thefe fpurious characters are now almoft naturalized into the language, by long ufe, and the hurry of bufinefs: for which reafon I have given in the Appendix fpecimens of the moft common.

The Shanfcrit, or facred language of Hindoftan, from whence the dialect of Bengal immediately proceeds, is fuppofed by its profeffors to be the moft antient and moft excellent in the world. They affert that it exceeds every other language in the number of its letters, and efteem this excefs as an incontrovertible argument of its antiquity and fuperiority.

The Bengal Alphabet, like that of the Shanfcrit, confifts of

FIFTY letters, in the following order.

FIRST SERIES.

অ *o*	আ aa	ই *ee*	ঈ ee
উ *oo*	ঊ oo	ঋ ree	ৠ ree
ঌ lee	ৡ lree	এ a	ঐ i
ও *o*	ঔ ou	অং ung	অঃ oh

SECOND SERIES.

ক ko	খ k,ho	গ go	ঘ g,ho	ঙ ng*oo-o*
চ cho	ছ ch,ho	জ jo	ঝ j,ho	ঞ gn*ee-o*
ট to	ঠ t,ho	ড do	ঢ d,ho	ণ aano
ত to	থ t,ho	দ do	ধ d,ho	ন no
প po	ফ p,ho	ব bo	ভ b,ho	ম mo
য jo	র ro	ল lo	ব wo	———
শ ſho	ষ ſho	স ſo	হ ho	ক্ষ khy-o

It

It is ufual with the Natives, whofe example I fhall partly follow, to defer all explanation of the firft fixteen letters of the alphabet, until they have thoroughly inftructed their pupils in the nature and ufe of the fubfequent confonants. The reafon of which is evident: for as every confonant is made to include in itfelf the fhort vowel neceffary to its enunciation, the firft thing requifite, is to account for this circumftance, and to fhew how the character which fhould denote this fhort vowel may be omitted without prejudice to perfpicuity and orthography.

The firft elements of every fcience muft be plain, fimple and eafy of perception: but more particularly thofe of letters; which, as they are generally taught in the early period of life, fhould be divefted of every fuperfluity that may diftract the attention, or clog the memory. This confideration feems to have been altogether overlooked in the elements of our own language, where we call the figure C, *fee*: and yet for the found *ka*, we write CA. In the fame manner G is pronounced foft like J in our alphabet; although the hard found of *Gamma* prevails in more than the proportion of four to five in its application. H, we denominate *aitch*, which does not fuggeft the moft diftant idea of an afpirate. To the letter Y we have affixed a name, which denotes neither the

vowel

vowel, nor the confonant: W is defined from its form only, not from its ufe; and Z *zad*, or *izard* is an appellation equally ufe-lefs and unintelligible.   The confequences of this perplexed fy-ftem are doubt, error and delay. In the languages of India thefe difficulties are greatly avoided, by giving to each feparate confo-nant the fame precife pronunciation in the alphabet, which it ever bears in compofition; and by annexing to it the imperfect vocal found which every attempt at utterance muft necellarily produce.

It is to be obferved, that in the Bengal alphabet, all the names of the confonants commence with the refpective confonants which they denote; as *ko, go, jo,* &c. Whereas in Englifh, fe-ven of them are preceded by a vowel: *ef, el, em, en, ar, efs,* & *ex.* It follows from hence, that the fhort vowel of the Bengalefe is invariably fubjoined to the confonant with which it is uttered, and never precedes: as 卡 and গ always ftand for k*o*, and g*o*, and in no cafe for *ok,* or *og.*

Moft of the Oriental languages are conftructed upon the fame principle, with refpect to the omiffion of the fhort vowel. The Hebrew had no fign to exprefs it before the invention of the Maforetic points. In Arabic it is rarely inferted, unlefs upon very folemn occafions, as in the *Koran.* In the modern Perfian it is

univer-

univerſally omitted: ſo to all the conſonants in the Shanſcrit language this ſhort vowel is an invariable appendage, and is never ſignified by any diacritical mark: but where the conſtruction requires that the vowel ſhould be dropped, a particular ſtroke is ſet under the letter, to regulate the pronunciation; a nicety, to which the inaccuracy of the Bengaleſe has not yet given place.

This inſeparable ſhort vowel is differently uttered in different languages, according to the genius of each; and perhaps in ſome degree to the organs of ſpeech in the various nations by which it is uſed. In the Shanſcrit it is called *Soor*, (or utterance) and throughout Hinduſtan has the ſound of the ſhort *e* of the French. In Arabic it is denominated *Futtah*, (or open) becauſe the conſonant to which it is added, ſtands open to the ſucceeding letter; and is ſignified by a ſhort line over the conſonant. This *futtah*, or *fatha*, is generally expreſſed in European languages by the ſhort *a*; but in utterance much more reſembles our *u* in *butter*. The Perſians call this vowel *Zeber*, (or above) on account of its poſition, which is the ſame as in the Arabic; and with them it has the ſound of *e* in *yes*; but in Bengal, where a very guttural accent prevails, it has a more open and broad tone, like the ſecond *o* in the word *chocolate*: as क ko, ग go &c.

The

The arrangement of confonants in this alphabet has a particularity, which I do not remember to have met with in any languages, but thofe proper to India: namely, that it is compofed
with a kind of regularity approaching to metrical exactnefs, which
renders it peculiarly eafy to the memory. Thus in the feries of
confonants beginning with the letter क ko, an evident rythm is
formed by the alternate fucceffion of the fimple and afpirated letters; and a cadence is introduced after each fourth, by the intervening nafal. In the latter part of the feries this nafal is omitted after the letter व wo: but in recital, a reft or paufe is
obferved, to make up for the deficiency.

I muft here inform the reader, that the vowels as ufed in
compofition, when joined with confonants, have a very different
figure from thofe, which he will have obferved in the firft feries
of the alphabet. Not to anticipate a general account of the precife found, and nature of them, I fhall here infert a table of the
forms of vowels in compofition, correfponding to thofe which
are initial or fingle; that the learner may not be at a lofs to read
fuch examples as immediately occur.

A

A T A B L E of the correſponding Vowels.

অ *o*   ক ko   (the included vowel)

আ aa	কা kaa		এ a	কে ka
ই ee	কি kee		ঈ i	কৈ ki or koͦi
ঈ ee	কী kee		ও o	কো ko
উ oo	কু koo		ঔ ou	কৌ kou
ঊ oo	কূ koo		অং ung	কং kung
	অঃ oh		কঃ koh	

ক   ko, has the ſound of *k*; as করুন koron to do.

খ k,ho, the ſame *k* aſpirated: as মাখন maak,hon butter.

গ go, is pronounced like *g* hard; as গমন gomon to go.

ঘ g,ho, the ſame *g* followed by an aſpirate, diſtinctly uttered. We have no ſound in Engliſh that reſembles it, but in ſeparate words; one ending with *g*, the next commencing with *h*, as in *tug*-*h*ard. In this manner is pronounced ঘর g,hor a houſe.

B

৯

ঙ ng*oo-o* This letter, when pronounced in the alphabet, has a ftrong nafal found like *nd* in the french word *'quand*. It is never found but in words of Shanfcrit origin, and then is conftantly compounded with fome other letter; and has the found of *un*, or *ung*, as in ঙ্ক un*ko* ,compofed of ঙ ng*oo-o* and ক *ko* in the word সঙ্কৰ fhu*nko*r a proper name.

চ ch*o*, the foft *ch* in *charge*: as চামৰু chaamroo a proper name. It alfo frequently bears the found of ʃ ftrongly uttered; as in চলন pronounced indifferetly chol*o*n or fol*o*n to go.

ছ ch,h*o*, is the fame letter afpirated; but in common difcourfe it is univerfally pronounced like ʃh in the word *dif-hearten*; as ছালিয়া ʃ haale*ee*aa a fon.

জ *jo*, pronounced indiscriminately like j or *z*; as জাব jaab*o* I will go; হাজাৰ haazaar a thoufand.

ঝ j,h*o*' is the former letter afpirated; as বুঝন b*co*j,hon to underftand.

ঞ gn*eeo*, the fecond nafal letter, never ufed but in Shanfcrit words, and in a compound form; when it bears a found approaching to *n* preceded by a nafal *g*; as পিঞ্জীৰা pe*e*gnjeeraa a birdcage.

ট *to*, the letter *t*, with a clofe, thick or obtufe found, produced by turning the tip of the tongue upwards to the roof of the mouth; as টাকা taakaa a Rupee.

ঠ *t,ho*, the fame letter followed by a diftinct afpirate like the *th* in *fweet-heart*; as ঠাকুর t,haakoor properly, a Deity, but ufed as a term of refpect and adoration.

ড *do, d* with the tongue inverted upwards, as in the preceding letters; as ডর dor fear. ডাকন daakon to call for. This letter has frequently the found of *r*, and fhould then have a fmall ftroke under it, thus ড় as বড় boro large. But in the hurry of writing the diacritical mark is commonly omitted.

ঢ *d,ho*, the fame *d* with a feparate afpirate; as ঢাকা d,haakaa written and pronounced *Dacca*, by Europeans, the name of a City.

ণ aano, the third nafal of the feries, with a found like *n*, as in ণাল aano, the name of the letter. Its ufe is confined to the Shanfcrit; and it is never diftinguifhed from ন no by the Bengalefe; which it is made to refemble both in form and found

a

as ষন্তোষ shontosh joy, pleasure.

ত to, the common *t*, as তুমি toomee you.

থ t,ho, the same letter, with a separate aspirate, as থাকন t,haakon to be, to remain.

দ do, the letter *d*; as দেখন dak,hon to see.

ধ d,ho, *d* with an aspirate; as বোধ bod.h knowledge.

ন gno or no, the fourth in the order of nasals; as নারী naaree a woman.

প po, the common *p*; as পলান polaano to run away.

ফ p,ho. In repeating the alphabet here explained, the aspirate of this letter is uttered distinctly, and subsequent to the *p*, like *p-h* in the word *ship-head*: But in common discourse it is usually pronounced like *ph* in Philip; as ফল Phol fruit, ফুল phool a flower.

ব bo, has the sound *b*; as ববিসন boreeshon to rain.

ভ b,ho, the preceding letter with an aspirate; as ভাল b,haalo b,haal*o* good.

স gm*o*, or m*o*, the fifth nafal; but has the found of *m* in common difcourfe; as মানুষ maanoofh a man.

য j*o*, has the found of *j*; as যুগল joog*o*l a proper name. The fame character with a ftroke under it thus য becomes the confonant *y*; as সয়ন fhoy*o*n accumbency, গিয়া geeyaa having gone. When য y*o* follows a vowel or an open confonant at the end of a word, it drops its own included vowel, and forms a kind of diphthong with the preceding vowel; as in the Englifh word boy: thus ভয় b,hoy fear, জায় jaay he goes &c.

র ঋ r*o*, is diftinguifhed from ব b*o* either by a ftroke acrofs or dot beneath it; as রাখন raak,hon to place.

ল ল lo, two forms of *l*, as বল bol ftrength. This letter in the common corrupted writing of modern Bengalefe is ufually confounded with ন n*o* in fhape; and not unfrequently in found: an example of which may be feen in the explanation of the next letter.

ব w*o*, in the Shanfcrit language is always ufed with the

found

found of *w*; but in the Bengalefe it is never diftinguifhẹd from ব bo either in form or utterance. The word *nabob*, ftrictly fpeaking, is novaab or nowaab. In Perfian it is written نواب *navaub* with a و *vau*, and in Bengalefe নবাব the fecond letter in the word being a wo; but by the Natives it is indifferently pronounced nobaab, *novaab*, and *lovaab*; as they generally confound ন no and ল lo, ব bo and ব wo. ব wo, when fubjoined to another confonant, is by the Bengalefe improperly pronounced *oo*; as দ্ব doo, প্ব poo, শ্ব fhoo, &c. compounded of দ do and ব wo, প po and ব wo, শ fho and ব wo.

শ fho, ষ fho, and স fo. The compilers of Shanfcrit grammars have been no lefs ftudious, than were the ancint Greeks in analyzing the elementary found of their feveral letters, and in diftributing them agreeably to the feveral organs by which they are uttered. Thus they have a clafs of *kungtee* or gutturals, of *taaloopee* or palatials, of *duntee* or dentals, of *ooſhtaanee* or labials, and of *naaſkaa* or nafals. They have even gone further, and allotted certain founds to the region of the brain; of thefe there are four: ঋ ree, ট to, র ro, and শ fho; which are called *moordhenee* or cerebrals.

I

I believe no other language ever contained a subdivision of the simple sound expressed by *sh*, but by the writers of Shanscrit শ *sho* is ranked under the cerebrals, ষ *sho* belongs to the palate, and স *so* is a dental. These letters are by no means interchangeable in the original dialect; but each has its own office, and peculiar usage. The modern Bengalese, equally careless and ignorant of all arts but those of gain, indiscriminately give the sound of *sh* to each of the three characters, and apply them indifferently, as chance or caprice directs; so that there is no possible difference to be observed in their pronunciation of শ *sho* and ষ *sho*, in the word বিশেষ *beeshash* increase; nor in that of স *so* and ষ *sho* in আস্বাস *aashwaash* reliance: they would indifferently write শুনন or সুনন *shoonon*, to hear; and so in other words: But ষ *sho*, they generally confine to the middle or end of a word, and seldom use it is as an initial.

The rules which the Indian grammarians have laid down for the meer orthography of the Shanscrit language would fill a volume; but as few or none of these are observed in the Bengal dialect, I have only taken notice of such as have some singularity to render them curious, or which are peculiarly characteristic of this ancient idiom.

হ

হ ho, a strong afpirate; as হাহাকার haahaakaar lamentation.

ক্ষ khyo, is a compound character added to the fett meerly to make the number of letters even, and the rythm of the alphabet compact; as there are but forty nine characters truly fimple and elementary. ক্ষ is derived from a junction of the two letters ক ko, and ষ fho; which having a very harfh found in combination, are foftened into ক্ষ khyo This letter when tranfpofed into the Perfian character, is frequently rendered by چ che, which is a collateral proof of its origin: Thus for khyotree (one of the four primary Hindoo tribes) the Perfians fubftitute chetree, লক্ষী lokhvmee a proper name, they write lechmee: And if we were to give to ক্ষ khyo, its original found of kfh, there would be but little difference between lechmee and lekfhmee. This letter is not much ufed by the modern Bengalefe, and is confined to Shanfcrit words; as পরীক্ষা poreekhyaa trial by ordeal.

I have already mentioned, that by the original ftructure of this language every confonant inherently poffeffes the fhort vowel on which its utterance depends; it is plain therefore on

this

this principle, that no two confonants could have been joined together, and fucceffively pronounced in the fame fyllable; but that a vowel muft neceffarily have intervented. As an expedient to remedy this inconvenience, a fet of diftinct characters was invented, called, ছল P,holaa, or adjuncts. They are certain fubordinate and fubfidiary figures, that may be attached to each of the confonants in the alphabet refpectively, to provide againft the too frequent recurrence of the internal vowel.

Thefe *P,holaa* are prefented in a diftinct feries or alphabet, confifting of eleven fubfervient marks or figns, for different letters; which are here joined to ক *ko*, the firft of the fingle confonants, and which may in the fame manner be applied to all the other letters.

The twelfth word of the feries (which feems to be added by the Bengalefe meerly to fill up the rythm) relates to another fubject, which will be explained in a fubfequent remark.

The reader muft remember, that the letter র *ro*, in its proper characters, is never joined to any other letter or adjunct; but its figure is entirely changed by a connection with other confonants, as will be feen in the following feries.

C

The

The twelve P, HOLAAS.

Figure.	Name.	Power.
ক্য	ky-*o*	ky-*o*
কুু	k*oro*	kr*o*
কুু	k*ono*	kn*o*
কুু	k*olo*	kl*o*
কুু	k*oo-o*	kw*o*, or fometimes koo.
ক্ষু	k*omo*	km*o*
কুু	kirr*ee*	kr*ee*
কুু	kill*ee*	kl*ee*
কুু	ark*o*	rk*o*
কুু	ungk*o*	ungk*o*
কুু	afhk*o*	fhk*o*
সিদ্ধি	fheedd,h*ee*	——————

The

These *P,holaas* may be comprehended by the following explanation.

ক্য kyo, is the letter য় yo added to ক ko, or any other consonant; as বাক্য baakyo a word, সৈন্য showinyo an army.

ক্র kro, is র ro subjoined to ক ko, or any other consonant; as কোধ krod,h anger, প্রথম prot,hom first.

ক্ন kno, in this figure ন no is joined to any other letter; as বিঘ্ন beeg,hno a calamity.

ক্ল klo, is ল lo added to any letter of the alphabet; as আমল aamlo acid.

ক্ব kwo, is ব wo added to another consonant; as দ্বিতীয়া dweeteeyaa second; নিশ্বাস neeshwaash breath: But it is frequently pronounced *oo*, and confounded with the vowel ও *oo* in its compound state; as they write দুই for দুই doo-ee two, শ্বনন for শুনন shoonon to hear.

ক্ম kmo, ম mo subjoined to any consonant; as জন্ম jonmo birth.

birth.

কৃ kr*ee*, is the mixt letter শ্রী r*ee* in compofition with any confonant; as কৃষ্ণ kr*ee*fhno the name of a Hindoo Deity. নৃপ nr*ee*po a Prince.

ক্ল kl*ee*, the mixt letter ল্য l*ee* fubjoined to a confonant.

র্ক ark*o*, is র ro prefixed to a confonant; as দর্পন dorpon a mirror. Ignorant writers erroneoufly double the letter to which this *arko Pholaa* is prefixed; as আশীর্ব্বাদ for আশীর্বাদ aafheerbaad prayer.

The Bengalefe ufually tranfcribe all the *P,holaas* at length, as connected feverally with each of the confonants; to make them more readily comprehended, and more eafily retained. As I am not writing to children, this trouble would be unneceffary, and fuperfluous; and I fhall content myfelf with concife remarks upon fuch as are difficult, or anomalous.

The *P,holaa* ungk*o* is compofed of the feveral nafals prefix ed in their order to their refpective confonants, each to thofe of its own feries; and where the chain is interrupted, the letter ঙ ng*oo-o* fupplies the deficiency.

Th

The *P,holaa* ঙ্ক *ungko* compleat.

ungko	ungk,ho	ungo	ung,ho	ung-*o-oo*
ungcho	ungch,ho	ungjo	ungj,ho	ung-*ee-o*
ungto	ungt,ho	ungdo	ungd,ho	ung-aano
ungto	ungto,ho	ungdo	ungd,ho	ungno
umpo	ump,ho	umb,ho	umb,ho	ummo
ungjo	ro	unglo	ungwo	————
ungſho	ungſho	ungſo	ungho	ungkhyo

Examples ; সঙ্কা ſhungkaa fear, চিন্তন cheenton to confider, কম্বল kumbol a blanket &c. ঙ্ক uncho is more frequently written in a contracted character, thus ক্ষ as পঞ্চানন punchaanon the title of a Hindoo Deity; literally the God with five faces. কার্য্যঙ্ক kaarjjuncho affairs.

The

The *P,holaa* མྐ aſhko ſeems calculated to ſhew the ſeveral changes of ཟ ſho according to the different conſonants with which it happens to come in contact. I ſhall give this *P,holaa* alſo compleat.

*a*ſhko	*a*ſhk,ho	*a*dgo	*a*dg,ho	ungtro
*a*ſcho	*a*ſch,ho	*a*bjo	*a*bj,ho	*a*ggyo
*a*ſhto	*a*ſht,ho	*a*bdo	*a*bd,ho	*a*haano
*a*ſto	*a*ſt,ho	*a*bdo	*a*bd,ho	*a*hungno
*a*ſhpo	*a*ſhp,ho	*a*dbo	*a*db,ho	*a*hmo
*a*hjo	ro.	*a*hlo	*a*hbo	
*a*tſho	*a*tſho	*a*tſo	*a*tho	*a*tkhyo

Excluſive of theſe ſeveral *P,holaas* which have been explained above, almoſt any two or three conſonants may be blended together,

gether, to provide for the omiſſion of the intervening vowels. In the Shanſcrit language their ſeveral forms eaſily unite and run together, to make one compound letter ; like two drop of quickſilver upon approximation. The rules for the proper formation of theſe mixt characters, which ſhew how to remove occaſionally ſuch as are not compatible, and to ſupply their places with others that admit an union, occupy a conſiderable part of the Shanſcrit grammar; but are never attended to by the illiterate and careleſs race of modern Bengaleſe : by whom propriety of diction and orthography is not even conſidered as an accompliſhment.

The compound letters may be formed by three methods : either by placing one letter immediately under another ; as দ্ভ domb,h cunning; or by blending two letters together, ſo as to make one character from their union; as বিদ্যা beedyaa a proper name ; or by making the firſt of the two conſonants much ſmaller than the other letters , as কম্পবান kompowaan trembling. This laſt mode ſeems to be the moſt common.

সিদ্ধি ſheedd,hee, called the twelfth *P,holaa,* is a word always prefixed to the claſs of vowels contained in the firſt Series of the alphabet, page the fourth. *ſheedd,hee* is part of a Shanſcrit ſentence

tence সিদ্ধি রস্তু ſheedd,hee roſtoo, which means *be it proper-ly performed.* And as theſe words are uſually prefixed to the claſs of vowels, that ſeries has obtained the name of *ſheedd,hee*

The S E R I E S সিদ্ধি Sheedd,hee.

সি	দ্ধি	র	স্তু
ſhee	dd,hee	ro	ſtoo
অ	আ	ই	ঈ
o	aa	ee	ee
উ	ঊ	ঋ	ঋ
oo	oo	ree	ree
ঌ	ৡ	এ	ঐ
lee	lee	a	i
ও	ঔ	অং	অঃ
o	ou	ung	oh

There cannot be a greater defect in the ſtructure of any language, than that the ſame letter or letters ſhould be applied to ſeveral different ſounds; and that a variety of different combinations of letters ſhould expreſs the ſame ſound. Theſe two circumſtances ſhould ſeem to comprehend almoſt all the poſſible faults

faults in orthography, and yet are fo common in the Englifh language, that I have been exceedingly embarraffed in the choice of letters to exprefs the found of the Bengal vowels; and am at laft by no means fatisfied with the felection.

But I am obliged to acquiefce in the application of the following vowels and diphthongs; of which, fuch as are printed in Italic characters, are to be pronounced fhort, and the reft long: but the found to be given to the correfpondent long and fhort vowels is precifely the fame; and differs only in meafure, or time.

o   aa   ee   oo   a   o   ou

o   is generally to be pronounced like the fecond *o* in chocolate; but fometimes rather broader.

aa   muft have the found of *a* in falfe.

ee   like *e* in he, or *ee* in deep.

oo   as *o* is founded in move, or *oo* in tooth.

a   in every fyllable where it occurs muft conftantly be pronounced like *a* in labour.

i   is always to have the found of *i* in trial.

o   is confined to the found of *o* in moft.

ou   muft be pronounced like *ou* in houfe.

D

In

In the Series *ſheedd,ſhee*, which has been inſerted above, the characters শ্রী *ree* and শ্রী *ree*, ৯ *lee* and ৯ *lee*, ſeem to be of a mixed nature, as comprehending both a vowel and a conſonant: They are accordingly applied ſometimes in the one capacity, and ſometimes in the other. In the Series of *P,ſholaas*, they held the place of conſonants, under the figures কৃ *kree*, and ক্ল *klee*. Here they are ranked among vowels, and not improperly, when it is conſidered, that each of them ſingly forms a perfect ſyllable, and cannot be connected, in the ſame ſyllable, with any vowel; which is directly oppoſite to the nature of a conſonant.

অ *o*, is always an initial letter, as অপমান *opomaan* diſgrace. *NB.* This letter cannot poſſibly occur in the middle or at the end of a word, becauſe its place is ſupplied by the ſhort vowel included in the preceding conſonant; as for কঅরঅন *k-o-r-o-*n they write করন *koron* to do.

আ *aa*, is alſo initial; as আগে *aaga* before. For the reaſon above mentioned the অ *o*, or firſt part of this letter, is always dropped in the middle, or at the end of a word

word after a confonant; as *baap* a father is written বাপ

and not বআপ

ই *ee,* as ইন্দ্র *eendor* the name of a Deity, দুই *dooee* two.

ঈ ee, the correfpondent long vowel.

উ *oo,* as উপর *oopor* above, বাউ baa-*oo* the air.

ঊ oo, the correfpondent long vowel; as উপরোধ *oopo*-

rod,h compliment.

ঋ ree, as in ঋন *reen* a loan.

ৠ ree, its correfpondent long vowel; which never occurs in

Bengalefe.

ঌ *lee,* is never found but in Shanfcrit words, and in a com-

pound ftate; as ক্লৃপ্ত *kleepto* appointed.

ৡ lee, is ঌ *lee* doubled and pronounced long.

এ a, as এই a-*ee* this.

ঐ i, as in the Shanfcrit word ঐরাবত iraaɩot an elephant.

৩

ও o, as in যা|ওন jaaon to go.

ঔ ou, as in ঔষধ ouſhod,h mediᴄine.

অ° ung, is of a compound ſpecies. In the Shanſcrit language it is called অনুম্বৰ onoſwor, and is there uſed as a ſub- ſtitute for rhe letter ম্ mo; but without its inherent vow- el. The mixture of the vowel and conſonant is here eaſi- ly diſcoverable; as the ſhort অ o is added only to mark that it begins the ſyllable. When a conſonant has the firſt place, the dot only is retained of ung; while the inhe- rent vowel ſupplies the place of অ o; as ব°শী bung- ſhee a flute.

অঃ oh, the laſt figure of this claſs, is called বিসর্গ wee- ſorg, and is marked by two dots, one at the top and one at the bottom of the line. In the Shanſcrit language it is a ſubſtitute for the letters ৰ ro and স ſo, which are uſed in the terminations of particular forms of declenſion &c. It has no peculiar ſound or utterance; but gives a certain forcible pronounciation (almoſt like an aſpirate)to the vowel which is immediately before it; as নৰ nere man, ৱনঃ nereh a man, in the nominative caſe.

The

This figure, as ufed in the Bengal language, has quite loft its original property, and is applied indifcriminately to any vowel at the end of a word, without even altering the tone or force of utterance; but fometimes feems to ferve for a mark to denote that the inherent vowel of the final confonant is not to be dropped; as যাব jaabo I will go, might by miftake be pronounced jaab, as it is now written; but when weeforg is added thus, যাবঃ jaaboh, the latter vowel is marked beyond the poffibility of omiffion.

The connected vowels are given in the following Series, by the Bengalefe called বানান baanaan, and in Shanfcrit দ্বাদশ মাত্রাঃ dwaadofho maatraah the twelve marks, or figns.

NAME	FIGURE & POWER		NAME
okaar	ক্ ko	কা kaa	aakaar
hrofweekaar	কি kee	কী kee	deerg, heekaar
hrofookaar	কু koo	কূ koo	deerg, hookaar
akaar	কে ka	কৈ ki or koi	ikaar
okaar	কো ko	কৌ kou	oukaar
onofwaar	কﹾ kung	কঃ koh	weeforgyo

The

The plain ſtroke to the left of the firſt ক্র *ko* is here put as the mark of the ſhort vowel inherent in the conſonant; but this is never uſed on any other occaſion. The ſtudent will obſerve, that altho' ſeveral of theſe ſhort vowels precede in poſition the conſonants to which they belong, yet in utterance they are ſubſequent, and hold the ſecond place in the ſyllable.

The word হুম্ব *hroſwo* ſignifies ſhort, and দীর্ঘ *deergh,o* means long. The ſyllable কার *kaar* is always uſed to denote the names of vowels. Thus *okaar* means the vowel *o*, hroſweekaar the ſhort vowel *ee* &c.

To avoid the hiatus which would be occaſioned by two vowels coming together without an intervening conſonant, a conſonant homogeneous to the preceding vowel is to be inſerted between them, (as in the golden canons of the Arabic) or one of the vowels is changed into its correſponding conſonant.

য *yo* is homogeneous to এ *a*, ই *ee*, and ঈ *i*.

ব *wo* is homogeneous to উ *oo*, ও *o*, and ঔ *ou*.

Thus they write গিয়া *geeyaa* for গিআ *gee-aa* having gone for দুতীয়া *doo-eeteeyaa* ſecond muſt be written দ্বিতীয়া *dweeteeyaa*.

But

But ই *ee* may *follow* every other vowel without the infertion of a confonant; as জাই jaa-*ee* I go, not জায়ি jaa*yee*; দুই doo-*ee* two, not দ্বি dw*ee* or দুবি doo*wee*, এই a-*ee* this, not এয়ি ay*ee*, ওই o-*ee* that, and not ওবি ow*ee*.

So ও *o* or আ *aa* may *precede* every vowel, except এ a, without the intervention of a confonant; as বাও baa-*oo* the air; লিখিলাও leek,heelaa-o I wrote, a corrupt form of tenfe, &c. But when এ a follows ও *o* or আ *aa*, it is always changed into য় *yo* without its inherent vowel; as in নয় noy is not, for নএ no-a, contracted from নহে no-ha; জায় jaay he goes, for জাএ jaa-a.

When the vowel ই i is connected with any confonant, thus, কি that confonant does not drop its own included vowel; as কৈল is to be pronounced ko-ilo he did, বৈল bo-ilo he fpoke; where each vowel retains its own power diftinct, which thus nearly give the found of quil*o*, bwil*o*.

In fome cafes ই *ee* has the found and properties of ই i, when it ftands next to an open confonant, with which it does not coalefce: thus the word হইল was, is pronounced hwil*o*,

or

or ho-ilo; as if it had been written হৈল

In many cafes, where the vowel আ aa immediately follows ই ee in the fame word, (as in the preterite participles ending in ইয়া eeyaa) ই ee is frequently changed into য yo, and united with the preceding confonant by the *kvo pholaa*; as চড়্যা choryaa for চড়িয়া choreeyaa having afcended; ছাড়্যা ch,haaryaa for ছাড়িয়া ch,haareeyaa having deferted.

I muft here remind the reader, that the letter ব wo has entirely loft its proper ufe and power, in modern Bengalefe; and even where it occurs in words of Shanfcrit origin, is now univerfally pronounced like ব bo; as বচন wochon a word, is always bochon, with the Bengalefe; অগ্নিবত ogneewot like fire, they call ogneebot: and fo in all cafes whatfoever. This ufage has reduced them to the neceffity of inferting the vowel ও o, or ঔ oo wherever the found of W is to be preferved: as for বানা they write ওয়ালা oyalaa; for খেবা khawaa freight, they fubftitute খেওয়া kha-oyaa and thus confufe all derivation and orthography.

In addition to thefe remarks, I fhall fet down a few of the

most

the moſt common contractions of letters, which are conſtantly uſed by all the Bengaleſe, as being more expeditious, as well as more elegant than a ſimple junction of the ſingle letters, whoſe office they perform.

কৃ kro, ſtands for কৃ the kirro *Pholaa.*

ঙ okto, is ত to blended with ক ko; its regular form is ক্ত

কু koo, ſtands for কু ko with hroſwookaar.

ঙু ungo, is compounded of ঙু ngoo-o with গ go ſubjoined.

জ্ঞ oggyo, is another figure for the *Pholaa* জ্ঞ

ম্য moo, is ম mo and ব wo compounded. The ſimple form is ম্ব

ষ্ণ oſhno, for ষ্ণ i.e. ণ aano ſubjoined to ষ ſho.

ষ্ঠ ſhoo, initial and medial, ষ্ঠ ſhoo, final; two figures for ষ্ঠ

ত্ত This figure ſtands for both ত্ত otto and তু too.

গু goo, is uſed for গু

হু hoo, ſtands for হু

হ্র ohro, is kro *Pholaa* ſubjoined to হ ho.

ত্র tro, ſtands for ত্র

রু roo, is uſed inſtead of রু

হ্ল ohlo, is ল lo ſubjoined to হ ho.

ণ্ড ondo, compounded of ণ aano and ড do.

E

হ্য *ohjo*, is হ *ho* and য *jo* blended together.

হ্ম *ohmo*, a compound of হ *ho* and ম *mo*.

স্তু *oſtoo*, is স *ſo*, and ত *to*, with hrofwcokaar fubjoined.

স্ত্র *oſtro*, is the letter স *ſo* compounded with ত *to*, and the kro *Pholaa*.

হু *joo*, ſtands for জু

গ্ধ *ogd,ho*, দ্ধ *odd.ho*, ন্ধ *ond,ho*, repreſent ধ *d'ho* ſeverally fubjuined to গ *go*, দ *do*, and ন *no*.

ৎ this figure is called অর্দ্ত *ordd,ho-to*, i.e. *ſemi-to*; for *ordd,ho* ſignifies *half*. It is uſed for the letter ত *to* without its internal vowel; and in the middle of a word is generally repreſented by ২ the numerical figure of *two*; as in বৎসৰ *botſoro* a year.

ৎয *otyo*, is the preceding ৎ blended with the *kyo pholaa*.

I ſhall now proceed to a few marks of reference commonly uſed by the Bengaleſe.

৭ This figure is always put at the top of every writing, and is meant as an invocation to Gonaſh, the Deity of Knowledge and Arts; it is called গনেশের আকড়ি Gonaſhar aak*oree*, or the crook of *Gonaſh*. So the Mahometans always begin with the letter ‎ا‎ *aleph*, as a token of the unity of God.

৺ chaandboondaa, is a mark put over certain letters to give them a very forcible nafal expreffion; as বাঁস baas a bamboo, to be pronounced *baangs*, with the nafal ftrongly uttered.

Eefhwor. ঈশ্বর is properly one of the Deities of the Hindoo Trinity. The name of God was fuppofed too holy to be inferted among the general clafs of words, and was therefore written at the top of the Page, and wherever this name fhould occur in a fentence, the mark here fpecified was put as a reference to it. The form ftill remains, but the ufage is degraded into a meer compliment: for in all petitions, or letters from inferiors to their fuperiors, the name of the perfon addreffed is now put at the top, and this fign of reference occupies the place in the body of the letter, where the name fhould regularly have been inferted.

শ্রী free properly fignifies profperity; and is prefixed to every name which they mean to mention with refpect; as শ্রীশ্রী রাম free free Raam. শ্রীশ্রী গনেশ free free Gonafh.

One or more of thefe Titles of Hindoo Deities is firft written on every piece of paper, as an amulet or charm, before any letter petition or other writing whatever, is committed to it. In the fame manner the Mahometans univerfally apply their *Bifmillah* (or, *In the name of God.*) as we formerly wrote *Emanuel* at the

top

top of letters, and ftill continue to commence a Ledger with LAUS DEO.

I fhall here infert a fhort fpecimen of the Bengal language and character as an exercife for the learner. It is an Epifode extracted from the Dron Porb, or fifth book of the Mohaabhaarot, the grand Epic Poem of India. Throughout this work I mean to confine myfelf to examples taken from Poetry only; as we are fure, that Verfe muft have coft the author fome time and ftudy in the compofition; and is therefore likely to be moft conformable to the true genius and character of the language: and the regularity of the meafure is a great check upon the ignorance, or carelefsnefs of the copyift.

I might obferve, that Bengal is at prefent in the fame ftate with Greece before the time of Thucydides; when poetry was the only ftyle to which authors applied themfelves, and ftudied profe was utterly unknown. Letters of bufinefs, petitions, public notifications, and all fuch other concerns of common life are necefsarily, and of courfe, written without meafure or rythm: I might almoft have added, without Grammar. But all the compilations dedicated to Religion, to Hiftory and to Morality, and all fuch works as are expected or intended to furvive the compofer, are invariably written in Verfe; and it is probable no other ftyle will ever be adopted.

মহা

মহাভাৰতেৰ দ্রোনপৰ্ব্ব মধ্যে এক অধ্যায়

Mohaabaarotar dronporbbo mod,hya ak od,hyaayo

><><><><><><><><> ><><><><><> >< ><><><><><><><><

মুনিঃ বলে সুন পৰিক্ষিতেৰ তনয় ।
জেমতে সাত্যকি বীৰ হইল পৰাজয় ॥

Mooneeh bola ſocno Poreekhyeetar tonoyo

Jamota Saatyckee beero ho-ilo poraajoyo

এক কালে বসুদেব পিতৃ শ্রাদ্ধ কৰে ।
নিমন্ত্রিয়া ভ্রাতৃ বন্ধু আনে সভাকাৰে ॥

Ak kaala Boſcodab peetree ſhraaddho kora

Necmontreeyaa bhraatree bondhoo aana ſobhaakaara

সোমদত্ত বাহ্লিক আদি আৰ পঞ্চানন ।
সাৰু শিশু আইন পাইয়া নিমন্ত্রন ॥

Somdot Baahleek aadee aar Ponchaanon

Saaloo ſheeſhoo aaeelo paaeeyaa neemontron

আইন অনেক ৰাজা নাহয় গননে ।
সভাকাৰে বসুদেব কৈল অভ্যর্থনে ॥

Aaeelo onak Raajua naahoy gonona

Sobhaakaara Boſoodub ko-ilo obhyort,hona

নানা

নানা বিধি আসনে বসিলা রাজা গলে ।
একে একে সভাকারে পুছিল কথনে ॥

Naanaa beedhee aaſona boſeelaa Raajaa gona
Aka aka ſobhaakaara pooch,heelo kot,hona

বসুদেব থুড়া সেনী সাত্যেকিৰ বাপ ।
সোমদত্ত দেখি তবে বড় হইল তাপ ॥

Boſoodab khcoraa Sanee Saatyokeer baap
Somdott dakhee toba boro ho-ilo taap

ডাকিয়া বলিল সেনী সুন সোমদত্ত ।
সভা মাঝে বৈস তুমি এ কোন মহত্ত ॥

Daakeeyaa boleelo Sanee ſcono Somdctt
Sobhaa maajha bo-iſo tcomee a kon mohott

আমা সভা নামানিস কোন অহঙ্কারে ।
পৃথিবিৰ মধ্যে কেবা নাজানে তোমাৰে ॥

Aamaa ſobhaa naamaanees kon ohungkaara
Preet,heebeer modhya kabaa naajaana tomaara

মর্যদা

মর্য্যদা থাকিতে কেনো নাজাহো ঙচিয়া ।
আপন সদৃশ স্থানে ঙচি বৈস গিয়া ॥

এত শুনি সোমদত্ত কোপেতে জনিল ।
অগ্নির ওপরে জেন ঘৃত ঢালি দিল ॥

সোমদত্ত বলে সেনি নাক্রিস গর্ব্ব ।
তোমার মহিমা জত আমি জানি সর্ব্ব ॥

কোন দোষে দোষী আমি কহত সত্তর ।
এত কটু ভাসা মোরে কহিস বর্ব্বর ॥

তোমা হইতে নিচ কেবা আছয়ে মানুষে ।
মোর অগোচর নহে জানিয়ে বিশেষে ॥

এতেক শুনিয়া সেনী অতি ক্রোধ মন ।
কোপে ডাক দিয়া বলে শুন সর্ব্ব জন ॥

এত অহঙ্কার হইল আরে দলাঙ্গার ।
পরনিন্দা ছিদু নাহি চাহো আপনার ॥

ইহার ঙচিত ফল দিব আমি তোরে ।
এত বলি কোপে সেনী ঙচিল সত্তরে ॥

সেনী

সেনী দেখি সোমদত্ত অচিন অথন ।
হুড়াহুড়ি মহা যুদ্ধ কৰে দুই জন ॥

তবে সেনী মহা কোপে ধৰে তাৰ চুলে ।
দেখিয়া হইল হাস্য জত সভা তলে ॥

কেশে ধৰি চড় মাৰে বজ্ৰুৰ সমানে ।
এক চড়ে দত্ত ভাঙ্গি কৰে থানে থানে ॥

তবে সভে অচি দুহা নিবাৰন কৈন ।
অভিমানে সোমদত্ত দেশেৰে চলিন ॥

সভা মধ্যে সোমদত্ত পাইয়া অভিমান ।
তপস্যা কৰিতে বনে কৰিল পয়ান ॥

দ্বাদশ বৎসৰ সেই কৈন অনাহাৰে ।
এক চিত্তে সোমদত্ত সেৱে মহেশ্বৰে ॥

তপস্যায় বস হইল দেব দিগম্বৰ ।
বৃষভে চড়িয়া আইল বনেৰ ভিতৰ ॥

শিব বলে বৰ মাগ সুনহ ৰাজন ।
এত বনি সোমদত্তে ডাকে পঞ্চানন ॥

ধ্যান

ধ্যান ভাঙ্গি সোমদত্ত দেখিল মহেশ ।
বিভুতি ভুসন অঙ্গ জটা ভাৰ কেশ ॥

আনন্দিত সোমদত্ত দেখিয়া চান্দৰে ।
বিবিধ পুকাৰে রাজা অতি স্তুতি কৰে ॥

সোমদত্ত বলে যদি হইনা কৃপাবান ।
এক নিবেদন আমি কৰি তোৰ স্থান ॥

সভা মধ্য সেনী যোৰে অপমান কৈন ।
জতেক ভুপাতিগন বসিয়া দেখিল ॥

অগিনবত অঙ্গে দহে সেই অপমান ।
এই নিবেদন আমি কৰি তোৰ স্থান ॥

যদি মোৰে বৰ দিবা দেব পসুপতি ।
মহা ধনুর্দ্দৰ হঙ্ক আমাৰ সন্ততি ॥

তার পুত্রে মোর পুত্র জিনুক সমৰে ।
রাজা গন মধ্যে জেন অপমান কৰে ॥

ইহা বিনু অন্য বৰ নাহি চাহি আমি ।
এহ বৰ মোৰে দেব আজ্ঞা কর তুমি ॥

F

হর

হর বলে বর দিলু সুনহ রাজন ।
তোর যুদ্ধ জিনিবেক সেনীর নন্দন ॥

প্রানেতে মারিতে তারে নাহবে সকতি ।
এত বলি অন্ত ধ্যান হইল পসুপতি ।

দ্বিৰ স্থানে সোমদত্ত পাইয়া এই বর ।
আনন্দিত হইয়া গেল আপনার ঘর ॥

শিব বরে ভূরিশুবা সাথেকি জিনিন ।
তার উপক্ষন এই তোমারে কহিন ॥

An EPISODE from the Mohaabhaarot.

Moonee ſaid,   'Hear, O ſon of Poreekhyeeto,
  'How the hero Saatyckee was overcome.
  'On a certain time Boſoodab celebrated his father's obſequies,
  'And aſſembled all his Relations and Friends by invitation.
  'Firſt Somdott and Baahleek, then Punchaanon;
  'Saaloo alſo and Sheeſhoo were invited, and came.
  'Every Raajaa attended, more than could be numbered,

                                          'And

'And Bofoodab refpectfully faluted them.

'All thefe Raajaas he placed on various feats,

'And to each of them by turns addreffed his difcourfe.

'But Sanee, uncle to Bofoodab and father of Saatyokee,

'Was much enraged to behold Somdott among them.

'He called to him, and faid, "Hear O Somdott,

"What arrogance is it to feat yourfelf in this affembly!

"By what prefumption haft thou forgotten to refpect us?

"Who in all the world does not know thee?

"While your honour is yet fafe, why do you not rife and depart?

"Be gone, and feat thyfelf among thy Fellows."

'Hearing this, Somdott kindled with anger,

'Like oil when caft upon the fire.

'And Somdott replied, "Vaunt not thyfelf, O Sanee!

"For I am acquainted with all thy excellence.

"With what crime am I defiled, tell me quickly,

"That thou holdeft this violent difcourfe with me, O Wretch!

"Who among men is of lefs account than thyfelf?

"Neither is this hidden from me; I know it well."

'Sanee when he had heard this was exceedingly enraged,

'And

'And wrathfully exclaimed, "Hear him, O ye people!

"Art thou become thus infolent, O refufe of thy family!

"Whilft thou defpifeft others, knoweft thou not thyfelf?

"Soon will I give thee the proper reward of fuch conduct."

'Sanee hearing this, ftarted up in a paffion,

'And Somdott when he beheld Sanee arofe immediately,

'So that a defperate ftruggle enfued between them.

'Sanee in great fury feized him by the hair,

'At which a laugh circulated through the whole croud.

'He held his hair, and ftruck him a blow like a thunderbolt,

'And with that fingle ftroke demolifhed all his teeth.

'Then all the company got up and feparated them;

'Somdott in confufion retired to his own country.

'Somdott being thus difgraced in the midft of the affembly,

'Retreated into the defarts to pafs his life in prayer.

'Twelve years he confumed in prayer and fafting,

'In finglenefs of heart calling upon the great Deity.

'The naked God was fatisfied with his mortifications,

'And mounting his Bull came into the defart.

'Sheew faid "Hear, O Raajaa, demand of me fome favour."

'In thefe words the Deity with five heads addreffed Somdott.

'Somdott

'Somdott ftarting from his contemplation, beheld the Deity,

'Whofe body was covered with holy afhes, and his hair clot-
ted in a thoufand knots.

'Somdott was much elated to behold the Divinity,

'And humbled himfelf before him with the moft reverential
falutations.

'Then Somdott faid, "If You will really be my protector,

"Permit me to offer you a fingle requeft:

"Sanee has difgraced me in a numerous company,

"And all the monarchs who fate there beheld my misfortune.

"My body burnt like fire at the ignominious ufage:

"And therefore I humbly prefent this petition.

"If, O Lord of life, you mean to fulfill my wifh,

"Grant that my fon become a mighty warrior.

"Let my fon conquer his fon in battle;

"As He put me to fhame in the midft of the Raajaas.

"Except this, I have no boon to demand ——

"Beftow this, O God! my only requeft."

'The Deity anfwered "Hear O Raajaa, the favour is granted.

"Thy fon fhall overcome the fon of Sanee;

"But his life it will not be permitted him to deftroy."

'Thus

'Thus fpoke the Lord of life, and vanifhed.

'Somdott having received this favour from the Eternal,

'Returned exulting to his own family.

'Thus by the help of the great Deity, Bhooreefhrobaa van-
quifhed Saatyokee.

'And this hath explained to you the circumftances of his fall.

––––––––––––

CHAPTER II.

OF SUBSTANTIVES.

Genders are the fi ft attribute of fubftantives, and are ufually divided into three clafles; the mafculine, the feminine
and the neuter; under which are included the fubordinate an d
compound genders. In the Shanfcrit language (equally refined
with either the Arabic or the Greek) thefe three diftinctions are
preferved in their common number and order.

পুংলিঙ্গ *poongleengo* is the mafculine,

স্ত্রীলিঙ্গ *ftreeleengo*   the feminine, and

নপুংসক *nopoongfoko,* or ক্লীবলিঙ্গ *kleewoleengo* the
neuter.

The Authors of this threefold divifion of genders and of their

pre-

precedence, appear to have confidered the neuter as a kind of *refiduum* refulting from the two others, and as lefs worthy or lefs comprehenfive than either: but this doctrine is liable to fome objections. For the neuter (or that order of fubftantives defined by this term) feems to be of a more extenfive quality and power than the reft; in fo much that I fhould hardly fcruple to call it a genus, of which the mafculine and feminine are but the fpecies. For from the whole clafs of fubftantives, fome are felected to be mafculines, and others to be feminines; and all which are not thus fpecified, remain as the others were previous to their felection, *neuter*.

In Latin and Greek we find many unaccountable refinements of gender, or rather unmeaning applications of a diftinction without a difference. It would baffle the moft able grammarian to affign a fatisfactory reafon why *pecus pecoris* fhould be neuter, and *pecus pecudis* feminine; and fo of a thoufand others. Common fenfe requires that all general terms fhould avoid fuch difcriminations; and we certainly muft allow the conftruction of thofe languages to be moft rational, in which *flocks* and *herds* are of no gender, but include animals of both. In the fame manner when individuals are mentioned indefinitely, it is abfurd to fpecify the fex. We fee an animal at a diftance; muft

we

we know whether it be a he-goat or a fhe-goat, before we
venture to pronounce that it is a *goat* ?   Yet this knowledge
muft be pre-fuppofed in Greek and Latin, or it muft be granted that the gender is there redundant and fuperfluous.

The propofition which I have here ftarted is particularly
connected with my prefent fubject; becaufe in the Bengal language there is a great number of general neuter names of animals &c. to which may be added at pleafure different terminations of fpecification, fubdividing the individuals of the clafs to
which they refer, into the fubordinate diftinctions of male and
female.

The terminations ufually applied upon this occafion are, আ
aa for the mafculine, and ঈ ee, or নী nee for the feminine:
thus from বাঘ baagh, which fignifies a tiger in general, are
formed বাঘা baaghaa a (male) tiger, and বাঘনী baahgonee
or বাঘী baaghee a tigrefs; from হরিন horeen a deer proceed হরিন horeenaa a buck, and হরিনী horeennee a doe.

If ঈ ee long terminates the mafculine, it is made fhort before
the fign of the feminine ; as হস্তী hoftee an elephant, হস্তিনী
hofteenee a female elephant,   সান্তিপুরী faanteepooree a
man inhabiting Saanteepoor,   সান্তিপুরিনী faanteepooreenee a
                                                      woman

woman of Saanteepovr.

It is not neceſſary that every noun comprehenſive of Sex ſhould be diſtinguiſhed by a particular termination, or mode of formation, expreſſly to denote its gender.

The Sex of human creatures, and the more general relations which they bear to each other, are of ſufficient conſequence to obtain different names, inſtead of modifications of the ſame name. Thus in almoſt all languages the diſtinctions of *man* and *woman*, *huſband* and *wife*, *father* and *mother*, &c. are ſignified by ſeparate terms. The ſame may commonly be ſaid of ſuch animals as are moſt connected with mankind: from hence *bull* and *cow*, *ram* and *ſheep*, *boar* and *ſow* &c. Thus in the Bengal language মানুষ maanoolho is a man স্ত্রী ſtree a woman পিতা peetaa a father, মাতা maataa a mother, পুরুষ pocroolho a huſband, নারী naaree a wife.

পুরুষ ছাড়িয়া নারী রহিবে কে যেনে

pooroolho ch,haareeyaa naaree roheeba kimona

"When the huſband is gone how ſhall the wife remain ?"

upon the ſame principal আড়া aaryaa is a bull, and গাই gaaee a cow &c.

In other caſes different forms of the ſame word are applied to diftingu fh the Sexes; and as all animals muft be of one Sex, it is generally fufficient that the feminine term only be marked by a provifional inflexion: hence ছাগল ch,haagolo a he-goat ছাগিনী ch,haagolee a fhe-goat ভেড়া bharaa a ram, ভেড়ী bharee a fheep কুক্কুড়া kookooraa a cock কুক্কুড়ী kookooree a hen; রাজহ°স raajhungfo a gander রাজহ°সী raajhungfee a goofe.

টল টল করে জল মন্দ মন্দ বায়।
রাজহ°স রাজহ°সী খেলিয়া বেড়ায় ॥

Tolo tolo kora jolo mondo mondo baay,
Raajhungfo raajhungfee khaleeyaa baraay.

"A foft breeze gently agitates the water,

"The gander and the goofe fport and fwim."

The fame form occafionally takes place even when human beings are concerned, in a local or confined relation; thus we ufe the word *Jew* in a collective fenfe, comprehending the whole people; but to exprefs a woman of that nation we muft add a fexual termination; as *Jewefs*: fo ব্রাহ্মন braahmon fig-nifies a *Bramin*, or in general any perfon of the braminical tribe; but ব্রাহ্মনী braahmonee a *Braminefs*, or woman only of that Sect.

এত

এত সুনি ৱামকৃষ্ণ হাসিতে নাগিল ?
ব্রাহ্মন ব্রাহ্মনীকে পুবোধ কৱিল ॥

Ato ſoonee Raamokreeſhno haaſeeta laageelo
Braahmon Braahmoneeka probodho koreelo
"Heaiing this Ramkriſhen began to laugh
"And ſatisfied the Bramin and Bramineſs."

In all circumſtances of this nature, the reader will find in the Bengal language a wonderful reſemblance to the Engliſh idiom, and turn of expreſſion.

In Shanſcrit, as in Greek and Latin, the names of all things inanimate have different genders founded on vague and incomprehenſible diſtinctions : as if there could be any reaſon for making Ætna feminine, which would not equally hold good with reſpect to Veſuvius or Caucaſus. But this ſeems to be the natural conſequence of connecting the gender of a noun too intimately with its termination. Had all inanimate ſubſtantives in Greek and Latin wanted theſe ſexual refinements, the form allotted to the neuter would have increaſed beyond its due proportion, and the ear have been tired with the perpetual recurrence of ſimilar ſounds: but it is ſurely more conſiſtent with nature, to make every noun *neuter* which is not the name of ſomething

thing neceffarily *mafculine* or *feminine*: and this is an invaiiable rule in the dialect of Bengal.

Of Cases.

A Shanfcrit noun, on its firft formation from the general Root, exilts equally independ int of cafe as of gender. It is neither *Nominative*, nor *Genitive*, nor *Accufative*, nor is impreffed with any of tnofe modifications, which mark the relation and connection between the fevei al members of a fentence. In this ftate it is called an *imperfect* or *crude* noun. Thus রাজন্ Raajon means Monarch; but implies neither *a* Monarch, *of* a Monarch, *to* a Monarch, nor any other predicament in which a Monarch can be fuppofed to ftand. To make a nominative of this word, the termination muft be changed, and a new form fupplied; as রাজা ra jna a King রানী raanee a Queen. Thus we fee that in the Shanfcrit at leaft, the nominative has an equal right with any other inflexion to be called a cafe.

Every Shanfcrit noun is capable of feven changes of inflexion, exclufive of the vocative : and theiefore comprehends two more than even thofe of the Latin. I fhall here give a fhort explanation of them, in the order which has been fixed for

them

them by their own grammarians.

1 The Nominative, or *agent* in a fentence; as রাজা রা জ্যতি raajaa raɟjyotee a King governs.

2 The *Paſſive* cafe, or fubject of the action; as দেব নমি dawung nomee I worfhip God.

3 The *Cauſal* cafe, pointing out the caufe *by* which a thing is done; as দোৱন কৃতু dawano kreetung, made *by* God; or the inftrument *with* which it is done; as দাত্রেন চিন্ daatrano ch,heennung cut *with* a knife: or the fub-ject *in* or *by* which it is fuffered; as অক্ষী কান okhynaa kaanoh blind *of* an eye.

4 The Dative, with the fign *to* or *for*; as দেবায় দত্ত dawaayo dottung given *to* God, ধর্মায় ভদ্রু dhormaayo bhodrung good *for* religion.

5 The Ablative, implying the fubject *from* whence anything proceeds; as দেবাৎ পাপ্তু dawaat praaptung received *from* God.

6 The *Poſſeſſive* cafe, called by us the Genitive; as দেবস্য গৃহ dawoſyo greehung the houfe *of* God.

7 The *Locative* cafe, definitive of fituation, and generally known by the fign *in*; as জলে jola *in* the water, গৃহে greeha

greeha *in* the houſe, তর্কে চতুর *torka chotooro* learned *in* judgement.

The Vocative in Shanſcrit is excluded from the number of caſes, as no inflexion is employed in its formation: but to the imperfeᄃt noun the ſign হে *ha* is prefixed; as হে রাজন *ha raajon* O king!

The Inflexions of which a Bengal noun is capable, are neither ſo copious noɪ ſo accurate; the terminations uſed for this purpoſe are four only, and conſequently we can reckon but five different caſes at moſt.

The nominative is not diſtinguiſhed by any rule of formation; for in moſt ſimple or abſtraᄃt terms, the crude noun of the Shanſcrit is adopted, without the inflexion which denotes the Shanſcrit nomɪnative; but for concrete ſubſtantives, names of agents &c. where the termɪnation undergoes a material alteration in the Shanſcrit, that alteration is generally uſed in the Bengal dialeᄃt; as রাজা *raajaa* a king, from the crude noun রাজন *raajon;* স্বামী *ſwaamee* a huſband, from স্বামিন *ſwaameen.* Example,

স্বামী বনিতার পতি স্বামী বনিতার গতি

Swaamee *boneetaar potee* ſwaamee *boneetaar. gotee*

"The

"The hufband is the Lord of the wife, the hufband is the
guide of the wife."

The Inflexion which moft ufually occurs in Bengal nouns is made by the addition of the letter এ a; as দোষে dofha from দোষ dofh a crime: মানুষে maanoofha from মানুষ maanoofho'a'man; which may be called the *Oblique cafe* in general, from its frequent ufe.

This termination is occafionally applied to five feveral cafes.

1 To the nominative (redundantly) as বীরে beera for বীর beero a warrior, *Vir*;

আমি যদি সেনাপতি হইব সমরে ।
তবে অস্ত্র না ধরিবে কর্ণ মহাবীরে ॥

Aamee jodee fanaapotee ho-ibo fomora

Toba oftro naa dhoreeba Kornno mohaabeera.

"When I fhall be General in the battle,

"Then Kornno *the great warrior* will not take up arms."

2 To the paffive or fubjective cafe: as যুধিষ্টিরে from যুধিষ্টির Jood-heefhteer, a proper name; as

যুধিষ্টিরে ধরি দেহ এই নিবেদন

Jood-heefhteera dhoree daho a-*ee* neebadon

"Seize and give me Jood-heefhteer; this is my requeft."

It

3   It ferves to convey the fenfe of the third, fifth and feventh of the Shanfcrit cafes; as বানে baana with an arrow গগনে gogona from heaven: মাসে maafa in the month: কলিকাতায় koleekaataay in Calcutta; as

চারি বানে চারি অশ্ব মারিল তখন

Chaaree baana chaaree ofwo maareelo tokhyon

"With four arrows he then ftruck the four horfes."

এইত শ্রাবন মাসে ধারা বরিসে গগনে

A-eeto fhraawon maafa dhaaraa boreefa gogona

"In this month fhraabon the rains fall from heaven."

and this its proper ufe and application.

4   It is added to the termination of the poffeffive cafe, to form the dative: as দ্রোনেরে Dronara, to Dron

আর রথ করি তবে দ্রোনেরে নইল

Aar rot,ha koree toba Dronara lo-ilo

"He then brought another carriage to Dron."

5   It is alfo employed to diftinguifh the vocative, and may either be prefixed or fubjoined:

Pre-

Prefixed, as এ নাথ তুমি মোরে করিলা পরাধিন

A naat,ho toomee mora koreelaa pcraadheen

"O master! you have reduced me to a foreign subjection."

Subjoined, as সুন নৃপবরে shoono nreepobora hear O Prince!
from নৃপবর nreepoboro a Noble or Prince.

The second or passive case of inanimate nouns is almost always the same as the nominative, and is very rarely distinguished by a change of termination.

আর বান এড় বীর পূরিয়া সন্ধান ?

দুশাসনর অঙ্গ কাটি করে থান থান ॥

Aar baan ara beer pooreeyaa sondhaan

Dooshwaasonar ungo kaatee kora khaan khaan

"The hero having well pointed his aim, shot another arrow,

"And cutting the body of Dooshwaason, hewed it in pieces."

In this distich the words বান baan, সন্ধান sondhaan, অঙ্গ ungo and থানথান khaankhaan are in the passive or subjective case.

The same construction also takes place occasionally even in proper names; as

H

ধরি

ধরিবার যায় দ্রোন বাজা যুধিষ্ঠির

Dhoreebaara jaay Dron Raajaa Jood, heefhteer

"Dron goes to feize Raajaa Jood, heefhteer."

But this cafe fhould be formed by the termination এ a

when the noun ends with a confonant, and by রে ra or কে ka

when it terminates with a vowel: as

বহুত বচনে কহিল অর্জুনে

Bohoot bochona koheelo Orjoona

"He addreffed much difcourfe to Orjoon."

সাত্যকিরে ভুরিশ্রবা কর পরাজায়

Saatyokeera Bhooreefhrobaa kora poraajaay

"Bhooreefhrobaa defeated Saatyokee."

আর দশ বান বীর কর্ণকে মারিল

Aar dofh baana beer Kornnoka maareelo

"The hero ftuck Korno with ten more arrows."

I have obferved fome few inftances, wherein this cafe is made
to refemble the dative in termination; as in the book called
Beedyaa Soondor;

বিদ্যা সুন্দরে নইয়া কানিকা কৌতুকি হইয়া
কেলাস শিথর উতারিল

Beedyaa

Beedyaa Soondorara loi-yaa kaaleekaa koutookee hoi-yaa
Ko-ilaas leekhora ootoreelo.

"Beedyaa having obtained Soondor (her lover) and Kaalee-
"kaa being made contented, arrived at the foot of Koilas
"Seekhor (a mountain)"

This fecond cafe, with its Shanfcrit termination, is not total-
ly loft among the Bengalefe; tho' the very perfons who ufe it
are utterly ignorant of the principles on which it is formed, and
of the grammatical reafon for which it is applied. All petitions,
letters &c. in the Bengal language, commence with certain cufto-
mary phrafes of compliment in pure Shanfcrit, of which the
Writer knows nothing more than the general purport; after
this compliment is conftantly inferted the fentence নিখিত°
কার্য্যঞ্চ আগ Leekheetung kaarjyuncho aaga, which fignifies "I have written the affair (i.e. the affair which is the fubject of the letter or petition) here beyond." The word in the
paffive cafe is কার্য্যঞ্চ Kaarjyuncho: the fyllable cho is an en-
c'vtic, added only to fill up the metre, (for the line is a verfe of
eight fyllables) the word without this termination is কার্য্য°
kaarjyung. the fecond Shanferit cafe of কার্য্য kaarjyo an affair.
The fame form occurs in the word নিবেদন neebadon a petition; which in the eftablifhed formulary for the commencement

of

of all petitions is written নিবেদনঞ্চ *neebadonuncho* for নিবেদন^৩ *neebadonung.*

The th rd, fifth and feventh cafes of the Shanfcrit are likewife frequently fupplied by the termination তে *ta*, which is added to the nominative, when it ends with a vowel, and to the oblique cafe when the laft letter of the n un is a confonant; as অগ্নিতে *ogneeta with* fire, from অগ্নি *ognee* fire. জলেতে *jolata with* water, from জল *jolo* water. ঢাকাতে *dhaakaata from* Dacca. রথেতে *rot,hata, in* a carriage, or *from* a carriage. ভূমতে *bhoomata on* the ground.

অগ্নিতে পোড়ায় সৈন্য দ্রোন বিদ্যমান

Ogneeta poraay fo-inyo Dron beedyomaan

"He deftroyed the army *with* fire n Dron's prefence."

জলেতে হইল পূর্ণ সংগ্রামের স্থল

Jolata ho-ilo poorno fungraamar fi,holo

"The field of battle was filled *with* water."

রথেতে চলিল গিয়া

Rot,hata choleelo geevaa

"He hafted away *in* the carriage "

মূর্চ্ছিত হইয়া বীর রথেতে পড়িল

Moor-

Moorchch'heet ho-iyaa beer rot,hata poreelo

"The hero becoming fenflefs fell *from* the carriage."

সারথির মুণ্ড কাটি পাড়িন ভূমেতে

Saarot,heer moondo kaatee paareelo bhoomata

"Having wounded the charioteer on the head, he felled him *to* the ground."

The fixth Shanf rit cafe, or peff ffive form of noun, is conftucted by adding the letter র ro to the nominative if it ends with a vowel, or to the oblique cafe, if the laft letter of the word be a confonant: as বনিতার boneetaar genitive of বনিত boneetaa a wife. স্বামীর fwaameer from স্বামী fwaamee a hufband. মধুর modhoor fweet, the genitive of মধু modhoo, honey. মানুষের maanoofhar from মানুষ maancofho a man. কৃষ্ণর kreefhnar from কৃষ্ণ Kreefhno the name of a Hindoo Deity. Example.

কামানের হড়হড়ি বন্দুকের দুড়দুড়ি সম্মুখ ব লের গড় হয়

Kaamaanar hoorohoo *ee* bondockar doorodooree fommeckha baanar gor hoy.

"There is a twanging of bows, and report of guns,

"furely there muft be a fortrefs of arms before me."

কৃষ্ণের বচনে পার্থ ধনু অস্ত্র নিন

Kreeʃhnar bochona paart,ho dhonoo oʃtro neelo

"At the words of Kreeʃhno the Vizier took up his bow
and arms."

Some nouns ending with vowels increaſe a ſyllable in all the
oblique caſes, by prefixing to the ſign এ a the conſonant correſpondent to their terminating vowel; as ভাইয়ের bhaaeeyar
from ভাই bhaaee a brother. পাণ্ডবের paandowar from
পাণ্ডু paandoo the name of an ancient Hindoo family: and this
form (tho' very ſeldom uſed by the moderns) ſeems moſt conſiſtent with the orthography of the language.

ভাইয়ের মরন দেখি সিন্দুবীর বেগে ?
হাথে গদা করি গেল অভিমন্যু আগে ??

Bhaaeeyar moron dakhee ſeendoobeer baga

Haat,ha godaa koree galo Oɔheemonyoo aaga

"Seendoobeer ſeeing the death of his brother, taking his
"Mace in his hand, haſted to Obheemonyoo."

হাহাকার সব্দ হইল পাণ্ডবের দলে

Haahaakaar ſobdo ho-ilo paandowar dola

"There was much lamentation on the part of the Paandoos."

The

The *dative* is diftinguifhed by the final এ a added to the genitive, as I have already remarked; thus

রাজারে কহিল বীর সুন নৃপবর

Raajaara *koheelo* beer *foono* nreepobor

"The hero faid *to* the Raja, hear O Prince!"

Various Interjections ferve to point out the Vocative, and they will be noticed in their proper place; at prefent I fhall only obferve that the particle রে ra is commonly ufed in this fenfe, and may be added either to the word with which it is immediately connected in conftruction, or to any other member of the fentence, either noun or verb, as the compofer finds moft convenient; an inftance of the latter mode appears in this hemiftych,

যাওরে রজনি তুমি মরিয়া

Jaa-ora rojonee toomee moreeyaa

"O night! perifh and depart from us.

where যাওরে রজনি jaa-ora rojonee is put for যাও jaa-o রজনিরে rojoneera go, O night. For an example of this interjection being joined to its immediate fubject, I fhall quote the following little poetical fong.

গীত

গীত

ভব সিন্ধু পাৰৰে কে যাবা ভাইৰে
হৰি নামৰ নৌকাখানি স্ৰী গুৰু কাণ্ডাৰি
বাহ বাহ বন্যা ডাকে দুই বাহু পসাৰ
চাঙ্গৰ নিতাইয়েৰ ঘাটে অদান থেবা বয়
কত অন্ধ অতুৰ তাৰা সব পাৰ হয়

Bhobo ſeendhoo paarora ka jaabaa bhaaeera

Horee naamar noukaakhaanee ſhree goorou kaandaaree

Baaho baaho bolvaa daaka dooee baahoo poſaaree

T,haakoor neetaaeeyar ghaata odaan khawaa boy

Koto ondho otoor taaraa ſobo paaro hoy.

An ODE.

'O Brothers ! which of you will croſs the ocean of the world?

'There is the boat of the name of *Horee*, (the Deity) Shree

Gooroo (our Tutor) is the pilot;

'He hath ſummoned us, crying out,' "row, row, and ſtretch
wide both your arms;"

——'In the port of *Neetaaee* T,haakoor (a famous Divine) we
pay nothing for the paſſage,

'And there all the lame and blind are ferried over.'

The

The particle হে ha, the fign of the Shanfcrit vocative, is frequently applied to Bengal nouns in the fame fenfe; as

নাগৰহে গিয়াছিনাম নগৰেৰ হাটে

Nagorha geeyaach'heelaam nogorar haata

"O Naagor, I have been to the market at the City."

The Vocative is alfo expreffed by the crude noun, and by the nominative cafe of the Shanfcrit indifferently, without any interjection: as

হাসিয়া কহিল কৃষ্ণ সুনহ ৰাজন

Haafeeyaa koheelo kreefhno íconoho Raajon

"Kreefhno laughing faid, hear O King."

কর্ন্ন বলে মহা ৰাজা কর অবধান

Kornno bola mohaa Raajaa koro obodhaan

"Kornno faid, O great King, employ fage confideration."

As it may be curious to obferve at one view the connection and refemblance between a Shanfcrit and Bengal noun, and to trace in a corrupted language the gradual progrefs of deviation from its original fource; I fhall here infert a fubftantive declined after both methods, and ranked according to the Shanfcrit mode of arrangement, which I think at leaft equal in merit to the fyftem adopted by European Grammarians.

I

First Declenſion, a Subſtantive ending with a Conſonant.

SHANSCRIT.		BENGALESE.		
1	বানঃ baanoh	বান	baano	an arrow
2	বান° baanung	বানে	baana	an arrow
3	বানেন baanano	বানেতে	baanata	with an arrow
4	বানায় baanaayo	বানেরে	baanara	to an arrow
5	বানাৎ baanaat	বানেতে	baanata	from an arrow
6	বানস্য baanoſyo	বানের	baanar	of an arrow
7	বানে baana	বানে	baana	in an arrow
Voc:	হে বান ha baano	এ বান	a baan	O arrow

SECOND Declenſion,   a Subſtantive terminated by a Vowel.

	SHANSCRIT.		BENGALESE.	
1	অগ্নিঃ ogneeh	অগ্নি	ognee	fire
2	অগ্নি° ogneeng	অগ্নিকে	ogneeka	fire
3	অগ্নিনা ogneenaa	অগ্নিতে	ogneeta	with fire
4	অগ্নয়ে ognoya	অগ্নিরে	ogneera	to fire
5	অগ্নেঃ ognah	অগ্নিতে	ogneeta	from fire
6	অগ্নেঃ ognah	অগ্নির	ogneer	of fire
7	অগ্নৌ ognou	অগ্নিতে	ogneeta	in fire
Voc:	হে অগ্নে ha ogna	এ অগ্নি	a ognee	O fire

A

A third Declenſion might be formed for thoſe nouns which change their terminating vowel into a conſonant in the oblique caſe: as ভাইয়ে bhaeeya and পাণ্ডবে paandowa, oblique caſes from ভাই bhaaee a brother and পাণ্ডু paandoo a proper name &c. But theſe occur too ſeldom to require a ſeparate claſs: and occaſional anomalies are leſs fatiguing to a learner than a tedious multiplicity of rules.

The ſpecimens of declenſion here inſerted will have ſhewn, that Bengal nouns fall very ſhort of the powers and of the preciſion, which a greater variety of inflexion gives to thoſe of the Shanſcrit: yet the examples which I have already quoted from ancient books, prove that a ſingle oblique caſe has been uſed in many different ſenſes, like the dative in Greek, and ablative in Latin. But in modern language the ſyllable এ a or তে ta at the end of a word, is generally confined to the ſenſe of the *ſeventh caſe* as definitive of ſituation; and may conſtantly be rendered into Engliſh with the ſign *in*: as নগরে negora *in* the City ; ঘাটে ghaata *in* the Port; নামে naama *in* the name; মাসে maaſha *in* the month &c.

The third and fifth caſes are uſually ſupplied by certain particles anſwering to prepoſitions in Latin and Greek; and which compenſate for the defective ſyſtem of inflexion in Bengal nouns,

as

as well as in thofe of moft of the European languages.   The
ufe of thefe particles will be explained in a feparate Chapter.

OF NUMBERS.

In the preceding fection I have inferted the fingular number
only, as a fpecimen of declenfion, becaufe the Bengal language
has no proper form of dual or plural; both of which every
Shanfcrit noun contains, and each declined with feven cafes
like the fingular.   But as this work is by no means intended
to comprehend the whole grammatical fyftem of the Braminical
dialect, I have taken no notice of the great variety of its de-
clenfions, nor explained the difference of their inflexions as occa-
fioned by the difference of gender, as well as of termination.
I have alfo omitted to defcribe the modes of forming Shanfcrit
fubftantives of different genders from the fame root.   Every-
thing that immediately relates to my fubject, I fhall ufe my ut-
moft endeavours to infert;   but a compleat grammar of the
Shanfcrit would furnifh ample matter for a confiderable volume,
and prove a formidable tafk to the moft experienced philologer.

I have faid that Bengal nouns have neither *dual* nor *plural*
numbers, I may add that neither is wanted. The *dual* is found
in no modern language, and probably never exifted but in the
Arabic and its branches, in the Shanfcrit, and in the Greek.

That

That the idea of multitude is not confined to the plural number is clear beyond a doubt, becaufe fingular nouns are ufed in all languages with a collective fenfe, almoft as frequently as plurals: thus, *men love to ftudy*, and *man loves to ftudy*, are phrazes perfectly equivalent. So alfo we join to a noun in the fingular number an epithet of indefinite plurality, to convey a plural meaning: *many a man*, is written by the Bengalefe বহুত মানুষ boho̅t maanoofh. Perhaps it might be fafely urged that the fingular number has more occafion for an accurate fpecification than the plural: at leaft this is the only circumftance which can account for the extenfive ufage of the article, or reprefentative of unity in moft of the modern dialects of Europe.

In the Bengal language the fame form of noun ferves for the fingular and plural; fo that in an indefinite fentence no diftinction of number is obferved or provided for; as in the following verfes.

সৈন্য সৈন্য মহা যুদ্ধ হইল আচম্বিতে ।
রথি গন আইল চড়িয়া দিব রথে ॥
হস্তী হস্তী যুদ্ধ হয় মহা শব্দ করে ।
অস্ত্র আস্ত্রার যুদ্ধ হয় বিবিধ প্রকারে ॥

fo-inyo fo-inyo mohaa joodho ho-ilo aachombeeta

Rot,hee gono aaeelo choreeyaa deebyo rot,ha

Hoftee

Hoſtee hoſtee jcoddho hoy mohaa ſhobdo kora

Oſwo aaſwaar jooddho hoy beebeedh prokaara

"Troop with troop; on a ſudden there became a mighty battle;

"The Leaders haſted in their ſtrongeſt chariots:

"Elephant and elephant; the war raged with a terrible noiſe;

"Horſe and horſeman; the fight kindled in various conjunctures."

In this paſſage the words *troop, elephant, horſe* and *horſeman* &c. are taken collectively, and may be equally underſtood to be of the plural, or ſingular number. Where unity is to be ſpecified, the word এক ak*o* one, muſt be uſed like the article *a* or *an,* which latter I ſhould conceive to be a corruption of the word *ene.*   Example;

এক লাফে ধরিলেক তাহার চিকুর ।
এক চড়ে দন্ত গুলা করিলেক চুর ॥

Ako laapha dhoreelak taahaar cheekoor

Ako chora donto goolaa koreelak choor

"With a ſudden jump he ſeized his lock of hair,

"And with a ſingle blow ſhattered all his teeth."

Numerals may be joined to nouns in the ſingular number, without any confuſion of expreſſion, as we ſay fifty *horſe* (for *horſemen*) twenty *head* of cattle (for *heads*) ſo in Bengaleſe,

সত

সত সত হস্তী বীর মারে এক ঘায়

Scto ſoto hoſtee beer maara ako ghaay

"With one blow the hero ſtruck a hundred elephants."

Nouns of animation, and more particularly ſuch as relate to mankind, generally have their plural number diſtinguiſhed by the addition of certain words of amplification or multitude, which ſerve in a ſubordinate capacity, inſtead of a variation of form to the principal noun. Of theſe words, that which moſt commonly occurs in modern Bengaleſe is লোক lok a Shanſcrit word for a man, or in its collective ſenſe *people*; as

সর্ব লোক কহে যাও রাজার নিকট

Sorwo lok koha jaao Raajaar neekot

"All the people ſay, go before the Rajaa."

লোক lok when added to another ſubſtantive gives it a plural ſenſe; as পূজা projaa a peaſant, পূজালোক projaalok peaſants. তাঁতী taangtee a weaver, তাঁতীলোক taangteelok weavers.

But this uſage is very rare in books; in which plurality is moſt uſually ſignified by the word গন gono a multitude or army; as পন্ডিত pondeet, a learned Indian, or Pundit, পন্ডিত গন pondeetgono Pundits. সৈন্য ſo-inyo a troop, সৈন্য গন ſo-iny ſoi-*nyo gono* Troops.

নক্ষ নক্ষ সৈন্য গন বিনাসিল রনে

Lokhyo lokhyo ſo-ino gono beenaaſeelo rona

"He annihilated millions of Troops in the battle·"

বিদ্যার আভাস দেখি হইল বিস্ময় ৷
সকল পণ্ডিত গন হইল পরাজয় ॥

Beedyaar aabhaas dakhee ho-ilo beeſmoy

Sokolo pondeet gono ho-ilo poraajoy.

"On beholding the wonderful extent of his knowledge,

"All the Pundits were aſtoniſhed, and were overcome."

দল *dolo* is another word of the ſame purport and uſage as গন

gono; thus

ভয় পাইয়া পাণ্ডু দল সকল পলায় ৷
দুর্যোধন রাজা হইল আনন্দিত কায় ॥

Bhoy paaeeyaa paandoo dolo ſokolo polaay

Doorjodhon Raajaa ho-ilo aanondeet kaay.

"The Paandoos being terriſied, all fled,

"And Raja Doorjodhon was elated at heart."

Sometimes alſo গন *gono* and দল *dolo* are both applied together to give greater ſtrength to the expreſſion ; as

অর্জুনের

অর্জুনের রন দেখি বড় বিচক্ষন ।
ভঙ্গ দিয়া যায় তবে কুরু দল গন ॥

Orjoonar rono dakhee boro beechokhyon

Bhungo deeyaa jaay toba kooroo dol gon

" On feeing the wonderful battles of Orjoon,

" All the Kooroos fled from the battle. "

This form of plural may be ufed in the oblique cafe ; the fign of inflexion being added to the latter word only : as from কুরুগন kooroogono the Kooroos, may be formed কুরুগনে koorogona ; as

দেখিয়া কুরুগনে লাগে চমৎকার

dakheeyaa kooroogona laaga chomot kaar

" On beholding it, aftonifhment feized the Kooroos "

If the firft word had been in the oblique cafe, it would have been neceffary to underftand the latter in its full, and proper meaning ; as পাণ্ডু গন paandoo gono the Paandoos, পাণ্ডবের গন paandowar gono the multitude or army of the Paandoos.

পাণ্ডবের গনেরে জয়দ্রত কৈল জয়

Paandowar gonara joydrot ko-ilo joy

" Joydrot conquered the army of the Paandoos. "

K

গুন

গুনা *goolaa* is added to names of animals and things to form a plural, but not to thofe concerning mankind, as in this hemiftych from the Raamaayon or hiftory of Raam.

সিংহনাদ শব্দ করিয়া বানর গুনা আইসে

feenghonaad fhobdo koreeyaa baanor goolaa aaeefa

" On his making a noife like the lion, the apes approached."

Thus is ufed গরু গুনা *goroo goolaa* cows, from গরু *gorob* a cow; অস্ত্র গুনা *oftro goolaa* arms, from অস্ত্র *oftro* a weapon, &c.

দিগ *deeg* properly fignifies *a fide*; but when following another fubftntive, generally conveys a plural fenfe to it; efpecially in an oblique cafe; as পাসণ্ড *paafondo* a finner, পাসণ্ড দিগের *paafondo deegar* *of finners* or *on the part of finners*; as

সকল পাসণ্ড দিগর পাপ ক্ষয় হইল ?
নিতাই চৈতন্য আসি দরশন দিল ॥

fokol paafondo deegar paap khyoy ho-ilo

Neetaaee cho-itonyo aafee dorofhon deelo

"The faults *of all finner*s were obliterated,

"When *Neetaaee* and Choiton vifited them."

This

This word is more particularly applied to form the inflexions of the pronouns both perſonal and poſſeſſive, with which it is conſtantly uſed by the moderns in their converſation and correſpondence.

যুদ্ধতে পড়িযা সবে স্বর্গ পুরে জায়।
বন্ধু গনে তাহার দিগের না দেখি ওপায়॥

Jooddhata poreeyaa ſoba ſworgo poora jaay

Bodhoo gona taahaar deegar naa dakhee copaay.

"Thoſe who fall in battle all go to Paradiſe,

"But I ſee no remedy for their wives (or literally, *the wives on their part.*")

I muſt not omit that in the modern and corrupt dialeƈt of Bengal the ſyllable ্রা raa is ſometimes added to the nominative of a ſingular noun to form a plural; as ছান্যা ch'haalyaa a child ছান্যারা ch'haalyaaraa children.

CHAPTER III.

OF PRONOUNS.

নায়বাচ্য naambaachyo literally ſignifies *the implication of a name*, and therefore may be ſaid nearly to correſpond to the term *Pronoun*. It would be difficult to account for the variety

of

of words which have been allotted to this clafs by European grammarians; Perfonals, Reflectives, Demonftratives, Interrogatives, Indefinites &c. many of which cannot poffibly be taken for fubftitutes, or reprefentatives of nouns. Among thefe exceptions to clafs the figns of the fiift and fecond perfons, may perhaps be deemed too great an affectation of fingularity, or an unwarrantable licentioufnefs of criticifm; yet the authors of the Shanfcrit grammars univerfally confine the term naambochyo to the third perfon. The other two are ranked in the chapter of nouns, tho' diftinguifhed by a peculiar inflexion.

I and *thou*, the hinges upon which all difcourfe is turned, are not pronouns; they are perfonals, and nothing elfe: that is, they denote the prefence and perfonality of the collocutors, *I* being invariably the fign of the perfon who fpeaks, and *thou* that of the perfon fpoken to. They are not the fubftitutes for their names, becaufe thofe names could not be applied without circumlocution, preplex ty and abfurdity. They are not *pronouns*, becaufe they differ altogether in implication, power and extent from that which is moft affuredly a pronoun, the fign of the third perfon. *I* and *thou* teftify the act of difcourfe, *he* excludes from a participation in it: *I* and *thou* have no gender, *he* has both a feminine and a neuter. The firft and fecond per-

fonals

fonals fhould feem to be confined to rational and converfable beings only; the thiid fupplies the place of every object in nature: wherefore it muft neceffarily be endued with a capacity of fhifting its gender refpectively as it fhifts its fubject; and hence it is in Shanfcrit frequently denominated an *adjective*.

One of the demonftratives *hic* or *ille* ufually ferves for this purpofe; and generally the latter, which in Arabic has no other name than ضمير الغايب dhemeer el ghaayb *the pronoun of the abfentee*, for whofe name it is a fubftitute.

In moft languages where the verb has a feparate inflexion for each perfon, that inflexion is fufficient to afcertain the perfonality; but in Bengal compofions, though the firft and fecond perfonals occur very frequently, nothing is more rare than the ufage of the pronoun of the third; and names of perfons are inferted with a conftant and difgufting repetition, to avoid, as it fhould feem, the application of the words *he* and *they*.

The Bengal perfonals do not refemble thofe of the Shanfcrit in any of their inflexions: but as the cafes of the latter (in the fingular number) are fometimes applied in the more antient writings, I fhall here exhibit them in their own form and order.

The fecond perfon is always ranked before the firft, and the third before the fecond. Thus the roots of the firft and third

I   perfonals

perfonals are যুস্মদ্   অস্মদ্   *thou* and *I.*

	First Perfonal.		Second Perfonal.	
1	cafe.	হ্ব° thou	অহ্°	I
2		হ্বা|° thee	য়া|°	me
3		হ্বয়া| with thee	যয়া|	with me
4		তুভ্য়° to thee	যহ্য°	to me
5		হ্বৎ from thee	যৎ	from me
6		তব of thee	যয	of me
7		হ্বয়ি in thee	যয়ি	in me

Sometimes the form of the fecond cafe is হ্বা   যা| and the fourth and fixth তে   মে   Example.

জীবনে মরনে বাপি রাধাকৃষ্ণ গতি যম

"In life and death may Raadhaakreefhno be *my* Guide."

I fhall collect in this chapter all fuch words as ufually come under the head of pronouns in the European fyftem of grammar, whether declinable or aptotes. Such of them as are fubject to inflexion, have a regular but peculiar method of declenfion, which differs from that of fubftantives, both in the formation of the oblique cafes and in the general ufage of a plural number.

I

I shall divide them into three classes: the first comprehending all such words whose nominative singular ends in ই *ee*; the second containing those which terminate in এ a; and third composed of words incapable of inflexion.

And first of Nominatives in ই such as আমি I, তুমি you আপনি self, এই this, ওই that &c. Example.

এই ক্ষনে দ্রোন আমি বিনাশিব রনে

" At this juncture *I* will defeat Dron in the battle."

সেন বলে রাজা তুমি ভুবনে বিখ্যাত

"So-ilb said, Raajaa, *you* are famous in the world."

In the second or *passive* case the terminating ই *ee* of the nominative is constantly changed into আ aa; as আমা me তোমা you &c.

তোমা বিনে ধরে তারে নাহি হেন জন

" Except *you*, there is no one able to seize him."

The third, fifth, and seventh of the Shanscrit cases are represented by adding the termination তে to the *passive*; as আমাতে *with, from, by,* or *in* me; তাহাতে *with* &c. him, her, or it: as

তাহাতে অনেক সৈন্য করিলেক চুর

"with

"*With* it he cut in pieces all the troops."

It is to be remembered that altho' I have given the termina-tion ে as the fign of the third and fifth cafes of the pronouns, yet the moderns very feldom ufe either of them; but apply cer-tain particles anfwering to prepofitions when they would exprefs the fenfe of thefe cafes: a circumftance which I have already re-marked in the chapter of fubftantives.

The dative is formed by the termination রে ra added to the paffive cafe; as আমারে to me, তোমারে to you &c.

এই হেতু তোমারে আমি কহি এ রাজন

"On account of this I fpeak *to you,* O King."

The fyllable কে ka is fometimes fubftitued for রে in this cafe.

আনিয়াছ আমাকে আপনে আঙ্গা দিয়া

"You yourfelf ordered *me* to be brought hither."

NB. This dative cafe frequently fupplies the place of the paffive, like that of fubftantives; as in the preceding example and in this which follows.

বুঝা যদি আপনে আসিয়া করে রন ৷
তোমারে ধরিতে সে নারিবে কদাচন ৷৷

"If Brohmaa himself fhould come and fight,
"He fhall by no means avail to take *you* prifoner."

The *poſſeſſive* is made by omitting the final এ a of the dative; as আমার *of me,* or *mine;* তোমার *of you,* or *your's;* আপনার *of ſelf,* or *own;* as

মহা ধনুদ্ধর হঙ্ক আমার সন্ততি

"Let *my* fon become a mighty bowman."

আনন্দিত হইয়া গেল আপনার ঘর

"He went exulting to *his own* houfe."

Exclufive of the termination in তে ta, which is the fign of the feventh as well as of the third and fifth cafes, the pronouns poſſeſs a feparate form of inflexion peculiar to the *lccative* cafe; being the fame with that of fuch fubftantives as end in আ aa where the এ a final is changed into য় yo, as inftanced in the preceding chapter in the word কলিকাতায় from the nominative কলিকাতা In the fame manner to the paſſive cafe of the pronouns which always end in আ aa is added the letter য় yo; as আমায় in me তোমায় in you তাহায় in him &c.

তোমার দুঃথেতে আমার ঊপজিন দয়া ৷
অদিন্য করিব তোমায় দিয়া পদ ছায়া ৷৷

L "My

"My compaſſion is excited by your ſufferings,

"I will cauſe *in you* unceaſing bliſs under the ſhadow of **my**
feet."

বৈকুণ্ঠ ছাড়িয়া আমি আইনাম তোমার চাক্রি
সিন্নি দিয়া পুজ আমায় দুঃখ রবে নাক্রি ॥

"Having left the ſkies, I am come to your habitation.

"Give me ſweetmeats and worſhip me, and your troubles ſhall
not remain."

The nominative plural always ends in র া raa, and is formed either by changing the final ই *ee* of the nominative ſingular into র া raa; as আমর া *we*, from আমি I; তোমর া *ye*,
from তুমি *you*: or by adding আ aa to the poſſeſſive caſe; as
তাহার া *they*, from তাহার *of him*; আপনার া *ſelves*,
from আপনার *of ſelf*.   Examples.

সত্যে কহ নারী আমর া পাইয়াছি ডর

"Speak truth, O woman, for *we* are afraid."

তোমর া সকলে থাক রাজার রক্ষণে

"Do *ye* all remain in defence of the Raajaa."

The ſame inflexion ſerves alſo for the paſſive caſe plural; as

তোমর া জতেক ভাই বিধি কেন চাক্রি চাক্রি

"*You* Brethren, howmany ſoever, *Beedhee* hath conſigned to
different places "

The

The other oblique cafes of the plural are expreffed by the feveral inflexions of the word দিগ joined to the fecond or fixth cafe of the fingular; as আমারদিগে আমারদিগের তোমারদিগের &c. an example of which has been already inferted in the fecond chapter.

In common difcourfe this plural termination দিগের is frequently contracted to দের as আমাদের of us তোমাদের of you &c.

After thefe general rules it may not be improper to give the declenfion of each pronoun feparate, with fuch remarks as they may refpectively require.

1ft. perfonal আমি I.

Singular.		Plural.	
1 আমি	I	আমরা	we
2 আমা	me	আমরা	us
3 আমাতে	with or by me	আমারদিগেতে	by us
4 আমারে	to me	আমারদিগের	to us
5 আমাতে	from me	আমারদিগেতে	from us
6 আমার	of me	আমারদিগের	of us
7 আমায়	in me	আমারদিগে	in us

2d. per-

2d perſonal তুমি you.

Singular.		Plural.	
1 তুমি	you	তোমা	ye
2 তোমা	you	তোমা	you
3 তোমাতে	*by* or *with* you	তোমারদিগেতে	*by* or *with* you
4 তোমার	to you	তোমারদিগেরে	to you
5 তোমাতে	from you	তোমারদিগেতে	from you
6 তোমার	of you	তোমারদিগের	of you
7 তোমায়	in you	তোমারদিগে	in you

It is to be obſerved that the vowel উ *oo* of the perſonal তুমি is changed into ও *o* in all its inflexions both of the ſingular and plural ; for which particularity there is no other th in the authority of eſtabliſhed uſage.

The inflexions of আমি and তুমি in the fourth and ſixth caſes of the ſingular, and in the nominative plural are common-ly contracted in poetry ; as

মোর	তোরে	for	আমার	তোমারে
মোব	তোব	for	আমাব	তোমাব
মোরা	তোরা	for	আমরা	তোরা

Examples.

তুমি যদি দয়া নাথ না করিবা মোরে ৷
এ ভব সাগর মাঝে কে তরাবে মোরে ॥

" If you, O mafter, will not take compaffion on me,
" Who will fteer me through this dangerous ocean ?"

এই ক্ষনে রথ মোর চালায় সত্তর ৷

" Now fwiftly drive my chariot. "

রায় বলে বাস্থা দিলে হইনাম পৃথোসী ৷
আমি পুত্র সম তোর তুমি আমার মাসী ॥

" Raay faid, you have given me a habitation, and I am your
debtor.
" I will be as your child, and you fhall be to me an aunt."

ইহার উচিত ফল দিব আমি তোরে ৷

" I will give you the merited reward of this conduct"

The word which properly fignifies *thou*, is তুই of which
তোরে and তোর above quoted, are probably inflexions ; but
as in Englifh we have altogether fubftituted *you* for *thou* in polite converfation; fo in Bengalefe, cuftom has eftablifhed তুমি
in the place of তুই both in books and difcourfe : nor is the latter
ever applied but in contempt or anger.

The nominative of the proper pronoun of the third perfon ends
in এ a, and is therefore deferred to another part of the chapter.

The word ইনি is fometimes ufed in difcourfe for the third perfonal *he*, and its inflexions are ইনা ইনাতে ইনাৰে ইনাৰ
ইনায় ইনাৰা &c. but I have never met with a fingle inftance of it in books.

আপনি *felf* is a reciprocal or reflective pronoun ; and is declined as follows.

	Singular.	Plural.
1	আপনি	আনাৰা &c. As the plurals of
2	আপনা	all thefe words are formed by the
3	আপনাতে	inflexions of দিগ and have no
4	আপনাৰে	difference or variation, I fhall not
5	আপনাতে	burthen the Reader with any more
9	আপনার	of them.
7	আপনায়	

The poffeffive cafe আপনাৰ is occafionally contracted to
আপন when prefixed to another fubftantive,   with which
it coalefces ; as

সকলে আপনভাৰে জানে

"He confiders all men in his own fituation."

The demonftratives are   এই or এহি this, and অই or
অহি that.

Singular.		Plural.	
1 এই	অই	ইহারা	ওহারা
2 ইহা	ওহা	&c.	•
3 ইহাতে	ওহাতে	•	•
4 ইহারে	ওহারে	•	•
5 ইহাতে	ওহাতে	•	•
6 ইহার	ওহার	•	•
7 ইহায়	ওহায়	•	•

Cuftom has eftablifhed that the অ a of এই fhould be con-ftantly changed into ই ee, and the অ o of অই into ও oo, in all the oblique cafes; and has alfo ordained that in all the words of this clafs, whofe nominative terminates in a pure vowel, the letter হ ho fhall be inferted before the fign of the oblique cafe; as ইহা ওহা &c.

এই and অই when coupled with nouns, do not change their cafe like the adjectives and demonftratives of Latin and Greek, but continue in the nominative, like thofe of the En-glifh; whatever inflexion the fubftantive to which they belong many have affumed; as

এই মত পুতিজ্ঞা করিল পুনঃপুনঃ

" To *this* effect he repeated his promife feveral times."

f

We

We muſt now proceed to the third diviſion, conſiſting of words whoſe nominative ends in এ a.

Some of theſe are of both claſſes; as আপনে the ſame as আপনি ſelf, এ a contraction of এই this : and others are confined to the preſent form only, ſuch as সে he, (the pronoun of the third perſon) জে who or *whoever*, (the relative and contional) and কে *who* ? (the Interrogative.)

আপনে and এ are nominatives, as well as আপনি and এই

Examples.

রূপা করি সেনাপতি হইবা আপনে

" You favouring our cauſe, ſhall yourſelf be the commander."

পঞ্চজন্য শ°থ কৃষ্ণ বাজান আপনে ?

" Ponchojonyo, the ſhell of Kreeſhno, ſounded of itſelf."

অবিচারে চোর বলেন এ কোন বিচার

" Without inveſtigation they pronounce me a thief, what juſtice is *this* ? "

N.B. As এই is contracted to এ ſo is হই to হ়

সে the pronoun of the third perſon, is the ſame in all genders, and is thus declined.

Singular.

Singular.		Plural.	
1	সে he, she, it.	তাহারা	they.
2	তাহা him &c.	তাহারা	them.
3	তাহাতে *by* or *with* him	তাহারদিগের	by them.
4	তাহারে to him.	&c.	&c.
5	তাহাতে from him.	.	.
6	তাহার of him.	.	.
7	তাহায় in him.	.	.

In all the oblique cases of this pronoun, the স *so* of the nominative is changed into ত in which particularity it resembles the pronoun of the Shanscrit.

All the words of this division, as well as that above quoted, add the syllable হা haa to their oblique cases; thus,

দূরে থাকিয়া তাহা দেখে সর্ব্ব জন

" All the people beheld *him* from afar."

But this addition is occasionally dispensed with in the inflexions of the fourth, sixth and seventh cases of the singular, and in the nominative plural, where a contracted form was assumed as was also observed in the cases of আমি and তুমি Thus they use তারে for তাহারে তার for তাহার তায় for তাহায় and তারা for তাহারা

M   Examples.

Examples.

অতয়েব তারে তুমি কর সেনাপতি ?

"Therefore do you conſtitute *him* the commander."

এক্‌লাফ্রে পড়ে তার রথের ঊপর ?

"With one ſpring he darted upon *his* chariot."

বনমানা গলে দোলে যনি শোভা তায় ?

"A chaplet of flowers waves upon his neck, *in it* was an orna-
ment of jewels."

দাস দাসী জত তারা পলাইয়া গেল ?
জত কিছু ছিল দূব্য বেচিয়া থাইল ॥

"Howmany ſoever male and female ſlaves there were, *they are*
all fled,

"And have ſold whatſoever they had for their ſubſiſtance."

সে and এ are ſometimes oppoſed to each other, inſtead of
the two regular demonſtratives এই and স্রই thus,

সে দেশে কি রস আছে এ দেশে তাহারা

"In *that* kingdom what are the pleaſures? In *this* kingdom
they are theſe."

সহ or স is the Shanſcrit pronoun. It is ſometimes uſed

for

for a demonſtrative in Bengaleſe; as

সহ চরিগন কয় কারে হিরা করে ভয়

"Thoſe damſels exclaim, whom does Heeraa fear?

যে is moſt commonly uſed in a conditional ſenſe, for *who-ever* and *whatever*; and like সে has the ſame form for all genders: thus,

যে জন আপনা বুঝে পরদুখ্থ তারে সুঝে।
সকলে আপন ভাবে জানে ॥

"Whoever well knows himſelf, by him is felt the calamity of "another; and he conſiders all men as himſelf."

This word is frequently doubled to convey more clearly a conditional meaning; যে যে *what what*; that is, *whatever*; as

কক্না করিয়া বলে রাজা যুধিষ্ঠিরে।
যে যে কথা বনিল নারদমুনি বরে।

" Raajaa Joodheeſteer weeping repeated,
"Whatſoever words the great Naarodmonee uttered."

যে is alſo the relative *qui* of the Latin, and agrees with সে like the antecedent *is*; as

যে বিধি করিন চাঁদে রাহুর আহার।
সেই বুঝি ঘটাইন সন্যাসী তাহার ॥

" Beedhee

" *Beedhee*, *who* made the moon the food of the Raah*oo*,

" I know *he* brought the Sonyaa*f*ee to her."

যে has the fame mode of inflexion   as   সে thus, ɪ যে
2 যাহা 3 যাহাতে 4 যাহারে 5 যাহাতে 6 যাহার
7 যাহায় &c. But the fourth and fixth cafes are moft ufually
contracted into যারে and যার as

দিয়াছে যে কড়ি যারে দিগুন সুনায় তারে

" Whatever cowries he had given to each perfon, he charges

" him double the quantity."

কে is the interrogative *who* ? (but its neuter *what* ? is কি
and is indeclinable.)   Example.

আশ্বিনে এ দেশে দুর্গা পৃতিমার পূচার ।
কে জানে তোমার দেশে তাহার সঙ্খার ॥

" In the month aaf*ween* in this kingdom the Idol Doorgaa is celebrated,
" *Who* in your kingdom knows its figure?"

কে is declined like the preceding words : and like them has
its fourth and fixth cafes generally contracted into কারে and
কার as

কারে সেনাপতি করি কে করিবে পার

" *Whom*

"*Whom* muſt I chooſe for commander? *Who* will bear us
" through the ocean of the battle?"

কারে and কার are ſometimes ſubjoined to collective
words in a relative ſenſe, referring to the particular *perſon*, who
may have been previouſly mentioned in the ſentence or diſcourſe :
thus সভা is an aſſembly, সভাকারে implies the *perſons*
whom ſome aſſembly is ſuppoſed to contain. দুই is the numeral *two*, দুহা is a paſſive caſe derived from a modification
of it; and from thence comes দুহাকারে *the two perſons* (of
whom ſome mention has already been made.) Examples.

এক এক সভাকারে পুছিল কথনে

" He aſked *the perſons in the aſſembly* one by one ſome queſtion."

দুহাকার বানে দুহে হইল জর্জর

"By the darts of each of *theſe two*, (i.e. the perſons who have
been previouſly deſcribed as fighting together.) they were both
" pierced full of wounds."

The vowel এ the termination of the nominative caſe to theſe
pronouns, is frequently added to collective nouns, to give them
a perſonal or relative ſenſe : Thus from লোক people, is
formed লোকে *thoſe* people; from সভা an aſſembly, comes
সভে *thoſe perſons* who compoſe the aſſembly ; from সকল
ſignify-

ſignifying *all*, is made সকলে all *the people* : ſo এক means *one*, একে one *perſon*. দুই is *two*, but give it the termination এ a, and inſert the letter হ ho, as deſcribed when the nominative ends in a pure vowel, it becomes দুহে and ſignifies two *perſons*, or *the* two *perſons*. Examples.

সর্ব্ব লোকে কহে যাও রাজার নিকট

" All *thoſe* people ſay, go before the Raajaa."

সভাতে বসিয়া সভে করয়ে বিচার

" Sitting in the aſſembly, *thoſe aſſembled* conſulted together. "

দেখি কৃষ্ণ অর্জুন দুহে করে পুনিপাত

" Orjoon ſeeing Kreeſhno *they both* gave a ſalutation."

The word দুহে ſo compleatly aſſumes the character of a pronoun, that it becomes capable of all its inflexions ; and is thus declined : 1 দুহে 2 দুহা 3 দুহাতে 4 দুহারে 5 দুহাতে 6 দুহার 7 দুহায় Examples.

তবে সভেঞ্চি দুহা নিবারন কিল

" Then the people in the aſſembly aroſe and ſeparated *thoſe* " two *perſons*."

বানবৃষ্টি করে দুহে দুহার ঊপব ।
দুহাকার বানে দুহে হইল জর্জ্জর ॥

" *Thoſe*

" *Thoſe perſons* caſt at *each other* a ſhower of arrows,

" And by *each other's* darts they were *both* pierced full of wounds."

A repetition of theſe and other ſuch words, implies a diſtributive or reciprocal relation of perſons; as দুহে দুহে *each other*, or *both*; অন্যে অন্যে *each other*, from অন্য *another*; একে একে *one* by *one* or ſometimes *oneanother.*

একে একে সভাকারে পুছিল কথনে

" He aſked them all *one by one* ſome queſtion."

এক এক করে বীর বানের পুহার ।

" The Heroes attacked *each other* with darts."

অন্যে অন্যে সারথী কাচিন অস্ব রথ ।

দুহে মহা বনবন্ত দুহে মহা সত্ত ॥

" The charioteers reciprocally hacked *each other's* horſes and carriage;

"*Both* exceedingly ſtrong, and *both* exceedingly brave."

In all languages there are certain particles expreſſive of doubt as to number, quantity, perſonality, quality &c. and correſpondent reſponſives, ſimply reverſing the ſame indefinite terms, in which the antecedent was propounded; as *how many?* *ſo many.* *how much?* *ſo much.* *any one?* *no one.* *ſuch as, ſo* &c. Theſe are uſually denominated *indefinite pronouns,* and therefore

I

I have added them to this chapter. They are all aptotes in Bengalefe, as in Latin and Greek ; and in Shanfcrit are ranked with other indeclinable particles, in the clafs elegantly called নিপাত or *without leaves*, from their producing no inflexions.

কত koto *how many ?* quot;   তত toto *fo many,* tot.

কত দিন ছিন রাজা অরন্যের মাঝে

" *how many* days was the Raajaa in the defert ?

কত is often doubled, like the conditional যে to add energy to the expreffion ; as

কত কত বীর মারে বৃক্ষের পুহারে

" *What a number* of Heroes did he deftroy by the ftrokes of his club !"

জত is a conditional, and implies *how many foever.*

জত অস্ত্র এড়ে বীর তত পেনে কাটি

" *How many* darts *foever* the Hero flung, *fo many* he fhivered and threw down. "

কেহ *any one, fome one.* কিছু *anything, fomething.* কেহনা *not any one, no one.* কিছুনা *not anything, nothing.*

যায় রনে যোদ্ধাগন কেহ নাহি স্থির

" All the warriors go from the fight; there is not *any one* that
" remains unmoved."

অবস্য করিব যুদ্ধ নাহি কিছু ডর

"I will affuredly fight, for there is not *any* fear."

কোন কিবা and কেবা are interrogatives and fignify *who*, or *what?* and are indeclinable; as

করিব কোন ওপায়   "*What* remedy fhall I apply?

কিবা রূপ কিবা গুন কহিলেক ভাট

" Bhaat faid, *what* beauty *what* wifdom !

নিজ is an indeclinable poffeffive fignifying *own*, (*proprius*) and is joined to any other noun, in a reflective fenfe referring to the leading fubftantive in the fentence; as

এই রূপে রামাগীনঃ কহে পরস্পর ।

স্নান করি যায় সভে নিজ নিজ ঘর ॥

আনছলে পুন চাহে ফিরিয়া ফিরিয়া ।

পিঞ্জরের পাখি মত বেড়ায় ঘুরিয়া ॥

" In this manner the beautiful women talk to one another,

" And having bathed, each goes to her *own* houfe.

" Again with fecret glances they look at him repeatedly,

" Fluttering round and round like birds in a cage."

নিজ গৃহে প্রবেসিল রাজার কুমার

N

" The

" The fon of the Raajaa arrived at *his own* refidence. "

রাবনেরে বধি রাম সীতা আনে নিজ ধাম

" Raam having defeated Raabon, brought Seetaa to *his own*
" Palace. "

আপ্ত is another reflective aptote, which is always blended with its immediate fubject ; as

আপ্ত কথা ব্যক্ত কিনা এই দুখে মরি

" You have betrayed *our fecrets* ; and I die of·this injury."

Many other indeclinable particles are formed from feveral
pronouns by adding to them the terminations ন no, ত to, এক
ako, or হ ho; as কেন from কে জেন from জে তেন
the returning particle to জেন হেন from এ a contraction
of এই এত and এইত from the fame, জতেক from
জত এতেক from এত সেহ from সে &c.

I fhall conclude this fection with an inftance of each of them.
কেন *why* or *what ?* as

আজি কেন মন মোর করে ওচাটন

" Today why is my heart afflicted ?

রানীর দেখিয়া হান জিজ্ঞাসয়ে মহিপান
কেন কেন কহ সবিশেষ

"Be-

"Beholding the condition of the Raanee, the shepherd of the
"world said, *what what* is this? tell me the whole of it."

জেন *as or like,* তেন *so or such;* as

মৃতু কালে জেন-ঔষধ নাথায় ।
তেন যত দুর্যোধন অজ্ঞানের প্রায় ॥

" *As* at the time of death a man refuses all medicine,
" *So* Doorjodhon became almost void of reason."

হেন *this;* as হেন কালে সাত্যকি উঠিল ভূমে হইতে

" At *this* instant Saatyokee arose from the ground."

এত *this;* as এত বনি যুঝিতে চলিল বীর বর

" Saying *this*, the great Hero hasted to engage."

এইত *this;* as এইত শ্রাবন মাসে ধারা বরিসে গগনে

" In *this* month Shraabon the rain falls from heaven."

জতেক *howmany soever ;* as

জতেক দেখিয়া পুত্র পৌত্র পরিবার ।
কেহ কার নহে পার্থ সকল সংহার ॥

" *Howmany soever* children, grandchildern and relations I saw,
" O Paart,ho ! there are none of them left, they are all slain. "

এতেক *this;* as

এতেক সুনিয়া সেনী অতি ক্রোধ মন ।
কোপে ডাক দিয়া বলে সুন সর্ব জন ॥

" Having heard *this*, Sanee much enraged,

" Exclaimed in great anger, Hear O all ye people ! "

সেহ *that* ; as

ধনু যদি কাটা গেন অন্য ধনু নয় ?
সেহ ধনু কাটি এড়ে দ্রোন মহাসয় ॥

" When his bow was broken he took another bow,

" But the valiant *Dron* shivered *that* bow alfo."

জ *jo* and ত *to* are frequently affixed to fubftantives in the conditional fenfe of জেন and তেন as জখন at what time
foever, (*when*) তখন at the fame time (*then*.) Example;

সেনী দেখি সোমদত্ত ঊঠিল তখন

" *Somdott* beholding *Sanee*, arofe *at the fame time*."

CHAPTER IV.

OF VERBS.

THE Shanfcrit, the Arabic, the Greek and the Latin verbs
are furnifhed with a fet of inflexions and terminations fo
comprehenfive and fo complete, that by their form alone they
can exprefs all the different diftinctions both of perfon and time.

Three

Three feparate qualities are in them perfectly blended and united. Thus by their root they denote a particular act, and by
their inflexion both point out the time when it takes place, and
number of the agent.

In moft of the modern languages of Europe, as in many of
the dialects of Afia, thefe feveral modifications of the verb require to be feparately defined by pronouns, particles and auxiliary verbs. In Perfian for inftance, as well as in Englifh, the
verb admits but of two forms, one for the prefent tenfe, and
one for the aorift; and it is obfervable that while the paft tenfe
is provided for by a peculiar inflexion, the future is generally
fupplied by an additional word, conveying only the idea of time,
without any other influence on the act implied by the principal
verb. It is alfo frequently neceffary that the different ftate of
the action, as perfect or imperfect, be further afcertained, in each
of the tenfes paft, prefent and future. This alfo in the learned languages is performed by other variations of inflexion; for
which other verbs and other particles are applied in the modern
tongues of Europe and Perfia.

Every Shanfcrit verb has a form equivalent to the middle
voice of the Greek, ufed through all the tenfes with a reflective
fenfe; and the former is even the moft extenfive of the two in

its

its use and office : for in Greek the reflective idea can only be adopted intranfitively, when the action of the verb defcends to no extraneous fubject; but in Shanfcrit the verb is both recipro-cal and tranfitive at the fame time ; as আপুপ° পচতি সূদঃ *a cook prepares bread.* আপুপ° পচতে সূদঃ a cook prepares bread *for himfelf.* The fimple tranfitive is called in Shanfcrit পরস্মৈ পদ Porofmai pod ; the reflective আত্মনে পদ Aatmonee pod.

The verbs of the Englifh, however deficient of inflexions, have a very copious ftock of auxiliaries : exclufive of thofe which are common to moft languages, the ufage of the word *to do* in its prefent and paft tenfes, joined to infinitives or verbal nouns is peculiar to our idiom, to the Perfian, and to the Bengalefe. In the latter the verb করন *to do* is ufed through all its tenfes as an auxiliary : thus they fay indifcriminately বরিসে *rains,* and বরিসন করে *it does rain ;* রনিলাম *I fought,* and রন কবিলাম *I did fight.*

As neither the Shanfcrit, the Bengalefe, nor the Hindoftanic have any word precifely anfwering to the fenfe of the verb *I have,* the idea is always expreffed by আমার স্থান আছি *eft mihi,* and confequently there is no auxiliary form for the

Bengal

Bengal verb correspondent to *I have* written; but the sense is conveyed by নিখিলাম or নিখিয়াছি

There is no occasion for the application of an auxiliary to the future and subjunctive tenses, as they are both provided for by separate inflexions of the simple verb; in which instances the Bengal verb has certainly the superiority over those of the English, which otherwise they seem greatly to resemble.

I shall first present a paradigm of the auxiliary verb, because it is necessary to the formation of various tenses in all the other verbs.

The verb substantive *to be* seems in all languages defective and irregular. In Shanscrit it is called অর্ধ ধাতুক *semi-verb*, because it wants the form for the reflective sense.

It may be curious to observe that the present tense of this verb both in Greek and Latin (perhaps I might add in the Persian) appears to be directly derived from that of the Shanscrit, for which reason I here insert it.

SINGULAR.		DUAL.		PLURAL.	
অস্মি	*I am*	স্বঃ	*we two are*	স্মঃ	*we are*
অসি	*thou art*	স্থঃ	*ye two are*	স্থ	*ye are*
অস্তি	*he is*	স্তঃ	*they two are*	সন্তি	*they are*

This

This verb in Bengalese has but two diftinctions of time; the prefent and the paft, the terminations of the feveral persons of which ferve as a model for thofe of the fame tenfes in all other verbs refpectively.

The firft Bengal auxiliary আছি *I am.*

Prefent tenfe.

Singular.		Plural.	
আছি	*I am*	আছি আমরা	*we are*
আছিস	*thou art*	আছ	*ye are*
আছে	*he is*	আছেন	*they are*

Paft tenfe.

আছিলাম	*I was*	আছিলাম আমরা	*we were*
আছিলি	*thou wert*	আছিলা	*ye were*
আছিল	*he was*	আছিলেন	*they were*

আ the terminating vowel of the fecond perfon plural of the paft tenfe, is frequently changed into এ and they write indifcriminately আছিলা and আছিলে *ye were*; as

জট টাকা দিয়াছিলে সব গুলি থোটা

" Whatever Rupees you gave are all defective."

The firft fyllable of the verb fubftantive আছি is always dropped, when joined in its auxiliary capacity to the participles

of

of other verbs; as কহিতেছি *I am speaking*, not কহিতে
আছি গিয়াছিলাম *I had gone*, not গিয়া আছি
লাম Examples.

যে নাজ পাইয়াছি কহিতে নাজ পাও

" The difgrace which I have fuffered is difgraceful even to be
" uttered."

আট পনে আধ সের পাইয়াছিনি

" Thou hadft purchafed half a feer for eight Pons."

The fame ufage occafionally obtains with the paft tenfe of
আছি when connected with adjectives, or other words, and
not fubfervient to the participle of another verb.

শিশু ছিনাম বৃদ্ধ হইনাম চিন্তিতে চিন্তিতে

" I was young, but became old by repeated anxiety."

But notwithftanding this inftance, the tenfes of the verb fubftantive হওন *to be* are moft commonly applied with fubftantives or adjectives, as thofe of আছি are with participles.

Of Conjugations.

The verbs of the Bengal language may be divided into three
claffes, which are diftinguifhed by their penultimate letter.

1. The fimple and moft common form has an open confonant
immediately preceding the final letter of the infinitive; as

O

করন *to do*, দেখন *to see*, চিনুন *to think*.

2. The second conjugation is composed of those words whose final letter is preceded by ও pure, (that is, with another vowel or an open consonant before it) as জাওন *to go* হওন *to become* পাওন *to acquire*.

3 The third class consists entirely of causals derived from words of the first or second conjugation, and is known by having আ for its penultimate letter ; as ডরান *to cause to fear*, or *to terrify*, from ডরন *to fear*; লিখান *to cause to write*, from লিখন *to write*; খাওয়ান *to make to eat*, from খাওন *to eat*.

The several tenses of each of these conjugations are formed exactly upon the same principle : the only difference consists in the mode of applying their diacritical terminations, and is contained in the following rule.

In the first and third conjugations the final ন *no* only of the infinitive is dropped, to make room for the signs of the tenses; while verbs of the second class throw away the two letters ও *o*, and ন *no*. Thus লিখি *I write*, from লিখন লিখাই *I cause to write*, from লিখান জাই *I go*, from জাওন হই *I become*, from হওন

The source or original stamen of a Bengal verb of the first conjugation must generally be sought for among the primary roots of the

the Shanſcrit, which never enter into compoſition. Thus ঢুরুক্ষ or ক্রু (called *kru* by Dupont) is the Shanſcrit root wh ch implies *the idea of action*, and from whence proceed both the verb *to do*, and alſo a great number of nouns expreſſive of different modifications of the ſame idea, all derived from the two radicals ক্র and ধ or র as কর্তা an agent, কর্ম an action কার্য্য an affair, কার a particle of agency ſubjoined to other words, &c.

From the Shanſcrit infinitive করন° is formed a Bengal word করন which, though in conſtruction it bear the ſenſe of a verbal noun, and be declined in the manner of a ſubſtantive, is always confidered by the more learned Bengaleſe as the *root*, or infinitive of their verb : and thus ſeems rather to reſemble the infinitives of the Arabic, than thoſe of the Greek or Latin ; as in the following inſtances, where মরন *to die* and জীবন *to live* are applied ſubſtantively for *life* and *death*, and aſſume the ſign of the oblique caſe.

মরনের কালে রাজা গোবিব ভাবিয়া ।
সর্গপুরি চলি গেন রথেতে চড়িয়া ॥

" At the hour *of death* the Raajaa reflected upon Goveend,(God)
" and mounted in his car went haſtening to Paradiſe."

জীবনে মরনে বাপি রাধকৃষ্ণ গতি মম

" In *life* and *death* may the paternal care of Raadhaakreefhno *be*
" my fupport !"

Veibs of the fecond conjugation are derived from fuch Shanfcrit roots as have only one confonant; and as it feems contrary
to the idiom of the Bengal language to admit óf monofyllabic
infinitives, the fyllable ওন is added to the Shanfcrit root to
make up the deficiency.

Thus from জা Shanfcrit *to go*, is formed জাওন Bengalefe; and from গা *to fing*, গাওন

From the verbal noun, as above def.ribed, I fhall deduce
the feveral tenfes ufed by the Bengalefe, and illuftrate the rūles
for each by f.lect exa n les.

The prefent tenfe ind. fi ite is formed by fubftituting the perfonal terminations applied in conjugating the word আছি for
the final ন of the infinitive in the firft and third conjugations,
and for ওন in the fecond; as from দেখন *to fee* comes দেখি
I fee, from জাওন *to go* জাই *I go*, and from ডরান *to*
terrify is made ডরাই *I terrify*.

Example.

অগ্নি বর্ন সব দেখি সঘনে আকাষ ।
দিবসেতে ধুম কেত করয়ে পুকাষ ॥

" *I see* all the Heavens as it were in a cloud of fire,

" The ſtar Dhóomkatoo diſplays its brightneſs in the open day."

সগথ স°গ্ৰামে পডি সর্গ জাই আমি ৷

এই পাপে ধনঞ্জয় জাবে অধোগামি ॥

" Falling in the line of battle I *aſcend* to Paradiſe,

" But thou, O Dhonongjoy, for this crime wilt go to hell."

The form for the participle preſent is the ſame with that of the firſt perſon of this preſent tenſe ; as দেখি *ſeeing* or I *ſee*, আসি *coming* or I *come* ; as

সরুবীর ভঙ্গ দেখি দোনের নন্দন ৷

অর্জুন সগথে আসি দিন দরশন ॥

" The ſon of Dron *beholding* the flight of the Kooroos, *coming*

" into the preſence of Orjoon, diſcovered himſelf!"

The firſt gerund or ſupine is formed from this participle, by adding to it the termination of the oblique caſe তে as কান্দিতে *in* or *by weeping*, মরিতে *in dying*, হইতে *in becoming* &c. Example.

কান্দিতে কান্দিতে রানী হইন মুর্ছিত

" *By repeated weeping* the Raanee became ſenſeleſs."

This gerund com.nonly ſupplies the place and the uſe of our in-

infinitive mood; for when two verbs come together, the second in conſtruction generally bears this form, and muſt be attended with the ſign *to* in tranſlation; as

বুঝিতে নাপারি প্ৰাননাথ এ আর কেমন পিরিতি

" I am not able *to conceive*, O maſter of my ſoul, what manner
" of affection this can be."

শিশু সঙ্গে বেরাইল রাখিতে গোধন ৷
বন মধ্যে বনৎকার কৈল নারীগন ৷৷

" He conducted the children *to tend* the cattle; but in the deſart
" he uſed violence with the women."

তপস্যা করিতে বনে করিল পয়ান

" He retired to the deſart *to pray*."

The ſame oblique caſe of the participle preſent, and ſome-times its nominative, is joined to the contracted form of the tenſes of the verb ſubſtantive আছি to make a definitive pre-ſent, and paſt tenſe; as লিখিতেছি I *write* or *am writing* (li-terally I *am in writing*) বলিছে *he ſays*, করিতেছিলাম I *did* or *was doing*, &c.

মালিনী বলিছে আমি দুঃখিনী মালিনী

" The Herb-woman ſays, I am but a forlorn peaſant."

It

It is also joined to the present tense of the verb চাহন *to be willing* to express a future of determination or desire &c, like the Persian خواہم as লিখিতে চাহি I *will* write, I am desirous to write, জাইতে চাহি I *want to go*, I *will go.*

The indefinite preterite is made by adopting for the infinitive termination the sign of the past tense of আছি as দেখন *to see* দেখিনাম I *saw*, নওন *to take* নইনাম I *took*, করান *to cause to make* করাইনাম

আমি দেখিনাম অপরূপ রূপের বাজার

" I beheld a most beautiful person, an assemblage of charms."

In the dialect of some particular provinces of Bengal the last syllable নাম of this tense is changed into নু or নাও in the first person : and the copyists adopt the alteration in their Books; as may be observed in the *Beedyaasoondor*, where নাও is almost constantly written for নাম as among a number of instances

রূপী কর রাধানাথ নইনাও সরন

" Befriend me, O Raadhaanaat,ho ! I have assumed thy protecti-
" on."

হর বলে বর দিনু সুনহ রাজন

" The God said, hear O Raajaa, I have granted the favour."

From

From this tenſe proceeds a ſecond gerund with an ablative form and ſenſe, and to be conſtrued with the ſign *in* or *from;* as সুনিলে *in hearing*, or more properly *in having heard* &c.

পাণ্ডব বিজয় কথা অমৃত নহরি ?

সুনিলে অধর্ম্ম হবে পরলোক তরি ॥

" The relation of the victories of Paandob is a river of the wa-
" ter of life.

" *In having heard it*, my ſins are pardoned and I am cleanſed
" among the Porolok." (the ſouls of the deceaſed)

রায় বলে চাতুরি কহিলে কিবা হবে

" Raav ſaid, what will be the event *of* thus *deceiving* ? "

The vowel য়া being added to the participle of the preſent tenſe forms that of the paſt ; as মরিয়া *having died* হইয়া *having become* &c.

This participle like the former is prefixed reſpectively to the auxiliary words ছি and ছিলাম to expreſs a farther diſcri-mination of the paſt tenſe. The firſt of theſe tenſes we may ſtyle the *perfect preterite*, and the latter the *preterpluperfect* ; thus জিনিয়াছি *I have conquered* গিয়াছিলাম *I had gone* &c.   Example.

আমি জে হই সে হই আমি জে হই সে হই !

জিনিয়াছি পনে বিদ্যা ছাড়ি জাব নাই ॥

" I am what I am, I am what I am."

" But as I *have conquered*, (in the conditions of the marriage)

" I will not go and quit Beedyaa."

নাগরহে গিয়াছিনাম নগরের হাট

" O Naagór, I *had gone* to the market in the city."

The second perſon of the imperative is formed from the infinitive, by throwing away the final ন as করন *to do* কর *do thou,* সিখন *to learn* সিখ *learn thou,* সিখান *to cauſe to learn* (i.e. *to teach*) সিখা *teach thou,* খাওন *to eat* খাও *eat thou.*

মহা বনবান ভীম কর সেনাপতি

" *Make* the mighty athletic Bheem your general."

যাওরে রজনি তুমি মরিয়া

" O Night, *do thou,* having periſhed, *depart.*"

The other perſons of the imperative reſemble thoſe of the preſent tenſe reſpectively: except only the third, which has a termination peculiar to itſelf, and unlike every other part of the verb. It is derived from the ſecond perſon by the addition of উক as জিন *conquer thou* জিনুক *let him conquer,* হ *be thou* হউক *let him be;* পড়া *fell thou,* from পড়ান *to cauſe to fall* পড়াউক *let him fell.* Example.

মহা ধনুদ্ধর হউক আমার সন্ততি

P

" Let

" *Let* my fon *become* a mighty Bowman."

The letter হ is fometimes added to the fecond perfons of the imperative and prefent tenfe, to give weight and energy to the expreffion. I conceive it to be a contraction of হে the fign of the Shanfcrit vocative fubjoined to the verb, which is a very common idiom of the Bengalefe.   Examples.

শিব বলে বর মাগ সুনহ রাজন

" The God faid, *hear* O Raajaa, demand fome favour."

যদি না করহ মোর বাক্যের পালন ।
তিগ্ন বানে থণ্ড থণ্ড করিব এখন ॥

" If *you do* not furely obey my words,

" I will immediately cut you in pieces with my fharp fcymetar.

ইতাম is the termination of the conditional or fubjective, which is added to the radical letters of the infinitive: as from ধরন *to feize* proceeds ধরিতাম *I would feize,* যাইতাম I *would go* from যাওন &c.

সেনাপতি আগে যদি করিতাম কর্ন্নরে ।
এক দিনে ধরিতাম রাজা যুধিষ্ঠিরে ॥

" If *I had* before *made* Kornno a general,

" In one day *I fhould have feized* Raajaa Joodheefhteer. "

পক্ষি হইয়া জন্মিতাম থাকিতাম বৃন্দাবনে ।
অবস্য কৃষ্ণের নাম সুনিতাম শুবনে ॥

" *Were I* a bird, *I would remain* in the woods of Braendaabon:
" furely *I fhould hear* in mine ear the name of Kreefhno."

The future is formed by adding the termination ইব to the
radicals of the infinitive ; as লিখিব *I will write,* কহিব
I will fpeak পাইব *I fhall acquire* &c.

কি কহিব সোভা রতি মন লোভা যদন
মুহিত লাজে

" How *fhall I defcribe* her beauty ! Rotee eagerly wifhes it, and
" Modon is envious and afhamed."

But often, in the fecond conjugation, the fign of the future
is contracted to ব as যাব *I will go,* not যাইব &c.
হব for হইব as

একা যাব বর্দ্ধমান করিয়া যতন

" *I will go* alone to Burdwan, upon mature confideration."

বিসয় আসয় বুঝি রাজ পুত্র হবা

" Beyond all doubt, I am convinced you *muft be* a Raajaa's fon."

From this tenfe feems to proceed the third gerund with the
fenfe of *for* or *on account of*, by adding the termination বার

as

as নিখিবার *for to write* করিবার *for to do.*

করিবার মানভঙ্গ কবি কহে কত রঙ্গ

" *For to dissipate* his passion, he used various kinds of verses."

It sometimes has the sense of a genitive; as

আসিবার কালে মিত্র নহিল দরশন

" At the time *of my coming* my friend was not present."

এ enclytic is frequently added to this gerund as well as to every part of speech.

সাজিয়া আইন সভে করিবারে রন

" They all came ready prepared *for to fight.*"

The third person singular of the future, and of the simple preterite frequently assumes the termination এক instead of the regular form; as কহিলেক for কহিল *he spoke,* হইবেক for হইবে *he will be.*

দশ বান বিন্ধিলেক কর্ণ্ণর হৃদয়

" *He shot* ten arrows into Kornno's body. "

কে বুঝিবেক এ ঘোর " Who *will understand* this " calamity ! "

The letter ক is one of the enclytics, and is subjoined to various tenses of verbs, as চ is to the accusative of substantives without

without any particular meaning, meerly to fill up the meafure of the verfe, or as a diftinction of dialect.

Negative verbs are formed by the particle ন or না prefixed or fubjoined to any of the tenfes; as

না জানি কি হইল রাজা যুধিষ্ঠির

" I *know not* what is become of Raajaa Joodheefhteer."

কি করি বলনা আন সুলোচনা কেমনে আনিব তারে

" You *tell me not* what I muft do, O my love with bright eyes,
" how fhall I bring him?"

নাহি the Shanfcrit negative is frequently applied in compofition for the regular Bengal word; as

দ্রোন বলে সুন রাজা বচন আমার ? ইহার বিনে যুক্তি আমি নাহি দেখি আর ॥

" Dron faid, O Raajaa attend to my word,
" Except this I *fee not* any other counfel."

When ন or না is prefixed to the verb fubftantive হওন the open vowel of the penultimate is ufually dropped in all the inflexions of the tenfes; as নহে inftead of নহয় and নহিন for নহইন thus in an inftance lately quoted.

আসিবার কালে মিত্র নহিন দরশন

" At

" At the time of my arrival, my friend *was not* vifible."

The Shanfcrit নাহি very often adopts the place as well as the form of this negative verb and particularly in the third perfon of the prefent tenfe.

নাহি ধন নাহি জন নাহিক স্বহায় ৷
কেমতে বিধা জঙ্গ না দেখি ওপায় ॥

" I have no treafure (*non eſt gaza*) I have no fervants, I have no
" affiftance,

" How fhall I perform this facrifice? I fee no method."

Paradigm of an active verb.

Prefent tenfe indefinite.

Singular.		Plural.	
করি	I do	করি আমরা	we do
করিস	thou doft	কর	ye do
করে	he doth	করেন	they do

Definite Prefent.

করিতেছি	I am doing	করিতেছি আমরা	we &c.
করিতেছিস	thou art doing	করিতেছ	ye are doing
করিতেছে	he is doing	করিতেছেন	they are doing

Simple Preterite.

করিনাম	I did	করিনাম আমরা	we did
করিলি	thou didſt	করিলা	ye did
করিল	he did	করিলেন	they did

Imperfect Preterite.

করিতেছিলাম	I was doing	করিতেছিলাম অমরা	we [were doing
করিতেছিলি	thou wert &c.	করিতেছিলা	ye were &c.
করিতেছিল	he was &c.	করিতেছিলেন	they &c.

Perfect Preterite.

Singular.		Plural.	
করিয়াছি	I have done	করিয়াছি আমরা	we &c.
করিয়াছিস	thou haſt done	করিয়াছ	ye have done
করিয়াছে	he hath done	করিয়াছেন	they have done

Preter-pluperfect.

করিয়াছিলাম	I had done	করিয়াছিলাম আমরা	we [had done
করিয়াছিলি	thou hadſt &c	করিয়াছিলা	ye had done
করিয়াছিল	he had done	করিয়াছিলেন	they had &c,

Singular.   Plural.

Future.

করিব	I ſhall or will do	করিব আমরা	we ſhall do
করিবি	thou ſhalt do	করিবা	ye ſhall do
করিবে	he ſhall do	করিবেন	they ſhall do

Conditional or Aoriſt.

করিতাম	I ſhould do	করিতাম আমরা	we &c.
করিতিস	thou ſhould'ſt do	করিতা & করিতে	ye &c.
করিত	he ſhould do	করিতেন	they ſhould do

Imperative.

. . . .		করি আমরা	let us do
কর	do thou	কর	do ye
করুক	let him do	করেন	let them do

Infinitive, or verbal Noun, করুন to do.

Participles.

Preſent, করি doing.   Paſt, করিয়া having done.

Gerunds and Supines.

করিতে করিলে করিবার in writing, from writing, to write &c.

The paffive voice is very feldom ufed by the Bengalefe : but is formed from a peculiar participle of the active verb, applied to the feveral tenfes of যাওন *to go*, exactly in the fame manner as the paffives of the Englifh are compounded of a participle, and the feveral tenfes of the auxiliary verb *to be*.

This paffive participle may be formed from infinitives of the firft conjugation, by changing the final ন into য়া as from নিখন *to write* নিখা *written*, কাটন *to cut* কাটা *cut*.

Example.

আছিল রাজার পুত্র কহিল তাহায় ৷
পড়িবা সকল পুথি জত লিখা যায় ॥

" There was a Raajaa's fon, to whom he faid,

" You fhall read all books whatever *that are written* "

ধ্বজ কাটা গেল তার অল্প অল্প সরে ৷
দুই বীরে হানাহানি সংগ্রাম ভিতরে ॥

" His ftandard *was cut* into pieces by the arrows,

" And there was a violent conflict between the two Heroes in

" the midft of the battle."

In verbs of the fecond clafs, the paft participle of the active ferves alfo for the paffive voice ; but few words of this conjugation are thus applied : দিয়া however fignifies both *having given*, (active) and *iven*; (paffive) as

কি কারন দিয়া গিয়াছিল সে টাকা

" On what account had thofe rupees *been given* ?

I have never feen verbs of the third conjugation ufed paffively.

যাওন *to go*, or in its auxiliary capacity *to be*, is irregular in the paft tenfes.

It is declined as follows.

Prefent tenfe indefinite	যাই	I go.
Definite prefent	যাইতেছি	I am going.
which is often contracted to	যাচি	
Irregular preterite	গেলাম	I went.
Preterimperfect	যাইতেছিলাম	I was going.
Perfect preterite	গিয়াছি	I have gone.
Preterpluperfect	গিয়াছিলাম	I had gone.
Future	যাইব or যাব	I fhall go.
Conditional	যাইতাম	I would go.

Imperative যা go thou, যাউক let him go, যাইয়ামরা let us go, যাও go ye. যান let them go.

Participles যাই going, গিয়া and যাইয়া having gone.

Tho' the irregular participle গিয়া is always ufed to form the paft tenfes of যাওন yet in other cafes, where the auxiliaries ছি and ছিনার are not applied, the participle যাইয়া regularly formed from the infinitive, not unfrequently occurs ; as

কাছে যাইয়া হাস্যা হাস্যা করয়েজি দ্বাসা

কে তুমি কোথায় ঘর কোন থানে বাস্য ॥

" *Having gone* near, and fmiled repeatedly, fhe makes enquiry,

" Saying who are you, where is your houfe, and in what place

" is your abode ?"

Gerunds and fupines যাইতে গেলে যাইবার in going,

from going, to go &c.

Other verbs fometimes fupply the place of যাওন in form-

ing the paffive voice, as পড়ন to fall, পাওন to acquire,

and হওন to be, compounded with the paffive participle:

nor is it contrary to the Bengal idiom to fay মারাপড়িলাম

or মারা পাইনাম or মারা হইনাম *I was beaten,*

altho' in books we very feldom fee any other mode of expreffi-

on than মারা গেনাম

দেওন *to give* is alfo irregular, and is made to refemble

a verb of the firft conjugation by throwing away the vowel এ

of its firft fyllable through all the tenfes, except fome perfons of

the imperative ; as দি *I give,* feldom or never দেই . দিনাম

I gave, not দেইসাম দিতেছি *I am giving,* not দেইতে

ছি দিয়াছি *I have given,* not দেইয়াছি &c.

Imperative দেও or দেহ *give thou,* দেউক *let him give*

দি আমরা *let us give,* দেহ *give ye,* দেন *let them give.*

হওন *to be,* নওন *to take,* &c, are regular as their firſt conſonant retains the inherent vowel through all the inflexions; thus হই *I am,* নই *I take,* not হি and নি হইনাম I *was,* নইনাম I *took,* হইতে হইয়া নইতে নইয়া &c.

পাওন *to acquire* is declined exactly like the verbs of the third conjugation, the vowel আ conſtantly preceding all the diacritical terminations; as

Preſent tenſe indefinite	পাই I acquire.
Definite preſent	পাইতেছি I am acquiring.
Paſt tenſe	পাইনাম I acquired.
Preter imperfect	পাইতেছিনাম I was &c.
Perfect preterite	পাইয়াছি I have acquired.
Preterpluperfect	পাইয়াছিনাম I had acquired.
Future	পাইব I ſhall acquire.
Conditional	পাইতাম I would acquire.
Imperative	পা or পাও acquire thou.
Gerunds and ſupines	পাইতে পাইলে পাইবার in

acquiring, from acquiring, to acquire &c.

In this manner verbs of the third claſs are univerſally conjugated; as করাই করাইনাম করাইব &c.

Examples.

রাবনেৰ বধি রাম সীতা আনে নিজ ধাম
করাইন পরীক্ষা দাহনে

" Raam killing Raawon brought Seetaa home to his own refi-
" dence, and *caufed her to perform* the ordeal with fire."

রথ চানাইয়া দেহ অতি সিঘ্রতর

" *Having caufed* the car *to haften*, give it me with all expedition."

নদিয়া সান্তিপুর হইতে থেয়ুড় আনাইব ।
নৌতন নৌতন জাতে থেয়ুড় শুনাইব ॥

" I *will caufe* the facred odes *to come* from Nodeeyaa in
Saanteepoor;
" I will *make you hear* odes conftantly new."

Some few verbs admit a contracted form in many of their
tenfes, particularly in the fimple preterites; as

for আসিনাম I came, they ufually put আইনাম
for করিনাম I made or did কৈনাম

But this remark moft properly belongs to profody, as thofe
words are generally fo contracted to fuit the rythm of the
verfe. Several inftances of this contraction may be found difperfed about this work: one will fuffice in this place.

তোমা ছাড়ি যাব যদি অন্যের নিকটে ।
তবে কেন তোমা নাগি আইনাম সঙ্কটে ॥

" If I fhould now forfake you and go to another,

" Why then *came* I through fo many dangers to vifit you ? "

Another very extraordinary contraction is that of নাপারি I *cannot*, (from the verb পারন *to be able*) into নারি as

ভাবিয়া করিতে নারি স্থির

" I *cannot* bring my reflections to any fixed point "

আমি কহিবার চাহি রাজারে রানীরে ।
কি বুঝিয়া করে মানা নারি বুঝিবারে ॥

" I am defirous to addrefs the Raajaa and Raanee,

" What they have heard that hinders me, I *cannot* difcover. "

I have alre dy fhewn that the verb fubftantive of the Shanf-crit very nearly refembles thofe of the Greek and Latin ; but perhaps it would not be fufpected that all the verbs in *mi* are formed exactly upon the fame principle with the Shanfcrit con-jugations, even in the minuteft particulars.

Thus from দা the root which fignifies *to give*, the prefent tenfe is made by adding the fyllable মি and doubling the firft confonant.   It is thus declined,

Singular.	দদামি	দদাসি	দদাতি
Dual.	দদ্ব	দদ্থঃ	দত্তঃ
Plural.	দদ্ম	দদ্থ	দদতি

To

To form the paſt tenſe, we muſt apply the ſyllablic augment as in the Greek ; and in faᵭt the very ſame letter: for অা in Shanſcrit anſ vers to *e pſilon* : thus it becomes অদদয় I *gave*.

The future has the letter স for its charaᵭteriſtic as we find in the Greek, and it omits the reduplication of the firſt conſonant as দাস্যামি I *will give*.

I cannot inſert the Greek form for want of types ; but the learned reader will not fail to be convinced of the ſimilitude. Let me add that the reduplication of the firſt conſonant is not conſtantly applied to the preſent tenſes of the Shanſcrit, more than to thoſe of the Greek.

The natural ſimplicity and elegance of many of the Aſiatic languages appear to be greatly debaſed and corrupted, by the continual abuſe of auxiliary or ſubſidiary verbs : at leaſt this inconvenience has evidently affeᵭted the Perſian, the Hindoſtanic and the Bengal idioms. The mode of expreſſion to which I allude, might have been a conſiderable embell ſhment to language, if applied with judgement and caution ; but the perpetual repetition has both deſtroyed the good effeᵭt of an occaſional relief to the ear by a ſtudied variety of phraſe : and alſo cebilitated the vigour of its periods, by a cumbrous addition of unmeaning ſyllables. The

The Shah nameh, the moſt nervous, the moſt accurate, and moſt poetical work ever compoſed by the Perſians, is be-come hardly intelligible to a modern reader from the great num-ber of original, pure and ſimple verbs with which it abounds. Theſe have long ſince given place to circumlocutory and unwiel-dy decompounds, formed of Arabic nouns, and the pliant auxili-aries کردن نمودن کردیدن or other ſuch un-emphatic ſubſtitutes. But it is not wonderful that the Perſians, who could formerly obliterate their own proper alphabet, in a ſuperſtitious adoption of the Arabic character, which by no means ſuited the genius of their language, ſhould now ſacrifice the purity and propriety of their phraſes to a habit of idleneſs, or an affectation of novelty.

The ſame circumſtance has equally prevailed in the Hindo-ſtanic and Bengal dialects. Of the latter the verb করন has ſwallowed up every faculty, and engroſſed every action to which the form of verb is applicable: and had it not happened that the infinitive of a verb is always conſidered and uſed as a noun, we might have attributed to the poverty of the language, or to a defect in its ſyſtem, that dull uniformity of expreſſion, which is now become its principal characteriſtic. We are however en-abled to trace the greateſt part of the original Bengal verbs from the roots of the Shanſcrit: and we may find them all in their

ſubfubftantive capacity applied to the feveral tenfes and inflexions of

করন ·

Thus by an unaccountable caprice the Bengalefe always exprefs the phrafe ' *I reprefent*' by নিবেদন করি from the
verb নিবেদন *to reprefent* ; as

এই নিবেদন আমি করি তোর স্থান

" *I make* this *reprefentation* to you."

And yet that they formerly ufed to conjugate this verb through
all its tenfes may be feen from the following inftance.

তোমা বিনে মোর দুঃথ নিবেদিব কায়

" To whom except yourfelf *fhall I reprefent* my mifery ? "

Every reader muft be difgufted at the exceffive ufage of this
compound form of verb, and it is on the excefs only that I
mean to criticize.

Every page of this work will afford frefh proofs of what I
have advanced ; I believe it will be found to proceed from a
lazy indulgence to the memory, and from a want of education
in the natives.

The number of pure verbs now ufed by them is very infuffi-
cient to the beauty and energy of a language ; but that they
once poffeffed a portion adequate to both purpofes may eafily be

R

com-

comprehended from the following lift, which I have fcrupuloufly confined to thofe only, whofe tenfes may be found in
authentic books.

I have felected fuch as moft immediately fpring from the
Shanfcrit Dhaats, which I have alfo inferted in a correfpondent
column; that while I fupport my prefent argument of the copi-
oufnefs of the Bengalefe, I may alfo bring additional teftimo-
ny of my former affertion refpecting its original derivation.

A fhort lift of V E R B S.

Shanfcrit Root & Infinitive.		*Bengal Infinitive.*	
অর্চ্চ	অর্চ্চন°	অর্চ্চন	to offer up.
অ°শ	অ°শন°	অ°শন	to partake.
অর্থ	অর্থন°	অর্থন	to require.
অঙ্ক	অঙ্কন°	অঙ্কন	to mark.
আন্দোল	আন্দোলন°	আন্দোলন	to fwing (intrans:)
আরূপ	আরোপন°	আরোপন	to fow, to plant.
আনী	আনয়ন°	আনন	to bring.
উৎতর	উত্তরন°	উত্তরন	to arrive.
কৃ	করন°	করন	to do.

ক্রন্দ	ক্রন্দন॰	কান্দন	to weep.
কম্প	কম্পন॰	কাঁপন	to tremble.
থণ্ড	থণ্ডন॰	থণ্ডন	to break in pieces.
থেল	থেলন॰	থেলন	to play.
থাদ	থাদন॰	থাওন	to eat.
থস	থসন॰	থসন	to drop off.
গঠ	গঠন॰	গড়ন	to make.
গৈ	গান॰	গাওন	to sing.
গদ	গদন॰	গাদন	to ram down.
গল	গলন॰	গলন	to melt. (intrans:)
গর্ব্ব	গর্ব্বন॰	গর্ব্বন	to be proud.
গন	গনন॰	গনন	to number.
গুন	গুনন॰	গুনন	to understand.
গর্জ্জ	গর্জ্জন॰	গর্জ্জন	to bellow.
গুঞ্জ	গুঞ্জন॰	গুঞ্জন	to hum, to buz.
জ্ঞা	জ্ঞান॰	জানন	to know.
ঘুর	ঘোরন॰	ঘোরন	to revolve.
চুব	চুম্বন॰	চুম্বন	to kiss.
চর	চরন॰	চরন	to graze (intrans:)
চিন্ত	চিন্তন॰	চিন্তন	to think.
চল	চলন॰	চলন	to go.

ছাদ	ছাদন°	ছাওন	to cover.
জি	জয়ন°	জিনন	to conquer.
জপ	জপন°	জপন	to recite the bead-roll.
জ্বল	জ্বলন°	জ্বলন	to burn. (intrans:)
জাগৃ	জাগরন°	জাগন	to be awake.
জৃ	জরন°	জরন	to be fick.
জীব	জীবন°	জীবন	to live.
ঝৃ	ঝরন°	ঝরন	to ooze out.
তাড়	তাড়ন°	তাড়ন	to beat.
ত্যজ	ত্যজন°	ত্যজন	to renounce.
ত	তরন°	তরন	to be ferried.
দহ	দহন°	দহন	to burn.
দংশ	দংশন°	দংশন	to bite.
দুহ	দোহন°	দোহন	to milk.
দুঃখ	দুঃখন°	দুঃখন	to be diftreffed.
দুল	দোলন°	দোলন	to fwing.
দা	দান°	দেওন	to give.
ধৃ	ধরন°	ধরন	to take, to feize.
ধু	ধুনন°	ধুনন	to bow cotton.
ধ্যৈ	ধ্যান°	ধ্যেয়ান	to meditate.
নিস্তৃ	নিস্তারন°	নিস্তারন	to be bleffed.

নিবৃ	নিবারন°	নিবারন	to forbid & to separate.
নী	নয়ন°	নওন	to take, to accept.
নিন্দ্	নিন্দন°	নিন্দন	to vilify, to defame.
নিবিদ	নিবেদন°	নিবেদন	to petition.
পঠ	পঠন°	পঠন	to turn. (intrans:)
পত	পতন°	পতন	to fall.
পদ	পদন°	পদন	to walk.
পৃ	পারন°	পারন	to be able.
পূজ	পূজন°	পূজন	to worſhip.
পরায়য়	পনায়ন°	পলান	to flee.
পুষ	পোষন°	পোষন	to cheriſh, bring up.
পৃ	পূরন°	পূরন	to fill.
পরামৃষ	পরামর্ষন°	পরামর্ষন	to conſult.
প্রশন্স	প্রশ°সন°	প্রশ°সন	to praiſe.
পড়	পড়ন°	পড়ন	to fall.
প্রবিশ	প্রবেশন°	প্রবেশন	to enter.
পচ	পচন°	পচন	to rot.
পত	পতন°	পাতন	to ſpread.
প্রসৃ	প্রসারন°	প্রসারন	to embrace.
প্রনয	প্রনমন°	প্রনমন	to ſalute.
ফল	ফলন°	ফলন	to bear fruit.

বস	বসন°	বসন	to fit.
বিন্ধ	বিন্ধন°	বিন্ধন	to bore, to pierce.
বন্ধ	বন্ধন°	বন্ধন	to refpect.
বর্ষ	বর্ষন°	বরিষন	to rain.
বন্ধ	বন্ধন°	বান্ধন	to bind.
বধ্	বধন°	বধন	to kill.
বর্ন্ন	বর্ন্ন°	বর্ন্নন	to extol.
বৃ	বারন°	বারন	to prevent.
বন্ধ	বঞ্চন°	বঞ্চন	to cheat.
বিদৃ	বিদারন°	বিদারন	to break (intrans:)
বিভজ	বিভজন°	বিভাজন	to diftribute in fhares.
বদ	বদন°	বলন	to fpeak, to fay.
বৃধ্	বর্দ্ধন°	বাড়ন	to grow.
বিতৃ	বিতরন°	বিতরন	to beftow.
বাদ	বাদন°	বাজন	to found as an inftrument.
বকি	বঞ্চন°	বঞ্চন	to bend.
ভী	ভয়ন°	ভয়ন	to fear.
ভৃ	ভরন°	ভরন	to fill.
ভাস	ভাসন°	ভাসন	to float.
ভজ	ভজন°	ভজন	to adore.
ভুজ	ভোজন°	ভোজন	to eat.

যজ	মজন°	মজন	to be ripe.
মহ	মহন°	মহন	to worſhip.
মান	মানন°	মানন	to mind.
মুষ	মোষন°	মোষন	to defraud.
ম্ৃ	মারন°	মারন	to beat.
যদ	মদন°	মাদন	to be intoxicated.
মৃজ	মার্জ্জন°	মাজ্জন	to ſcour.
মীন	মীনন°	মীনন	to join & to mix.
মৃগ	মার্গ্গন°	মাগন	to require.
ম্ৃ	মরন°	মরন	to die.
যা	যান°	যাওন	to go.
যাচ	যাচন°	যাচন	to want.
যুদ্ধ	যুদ্ধন°	যুদ্ধন	to make war.
রক্ষ	রক্ষন°	রক্ষন	to place.
ক্ৰষ	রোষন°	রোষন	to be angry.
রধ	রন্ধন°	রন্ধন	to cook.
রচ	রচন°	রচন	to compoſe.
লিথ	লিথন°	লিথন	to write.
নুম্হ	নুম্হন°	নুহন	to catch.
লিপ	লেপন°	লেপন	to plaiſter.
নঘ	নঙ্ঘন°	নঙ্ঘন	to leap over.

নভ	নভন°	নভন	to take.
লোক	লোকন°	লোকন	to fee.
নী	নয়ন°	নওন	to take.
নম্ফ	নম্ফন°	নাফ্ন	to jump.
নগ	ন্গান°	নাগান	to touch.
শী	শয়ন°	শয়ন	to fleep.
শান	শানন°	শানন	to whet, to grind.
শঙ্ক	শঙ্কন°	শঙ্কন	to fear.
শীল	শীলন°	শীলন	to be juft.
শিথ	শিথন°	শিথন	to learn.
শুষ	শুষ্কন°	শুকন	to dry. (intrans:)
সাধ	সাধন°	সাধন	to pacify.
সজ্জ	সজ্জন°	সাজান	to harnefs.
সান্ত্ব	সান্ত্বন°	সান্তান	to appeafe.
সাম	সামন°	সামন	to be quiet.
স্পৃহ	স্পৃহন°	স্পৃহন	to wifh.
স্মৃ	স্মরন°	স্মরন	to remember.
হন	হনন°	হানন	to cut.
হৃ	হারন°	হারন	to lofe in play.
হাস	হাসন°	হাসন	to laugh.

I have

I have not inſerted in this liſt many of the moſt common, and popular verbs of the Bengaleſe; which are either more corrupted in paſſing through ignorant hands, and therefore bear leſs analogy to the Shanſcrit: or which perhaps are really vulgar expreſſions adopted ſince the decline of learning.

I have not inſerted the cauſal verbs, which are derived from ſimple terms by the introduction of the letter আ. Their number would only have ſwelled my catalogue, without ſerving to any uſeful or curious purpoſe.

I have inſerted few ſuch verbs as are compounded of a particle prefixed or added to the Shanſcrit root. This claſs is very copious and comprehenſive, as the ſame word will have various and even contrary ſignifications according to the particles with which it is combined.

I have not inſerted ſuch words as in their formation from the Shanſcrit infinitives have altered, dropped, or exchanged their radical conſonants, except ſuch as are expreſſly convertible by the ſtrict rules of the Shanſcrit; as a ſimple conſonant for its correſpondent aſpirate, a ট for a ঢ or a র for a ঘ &c. Such alterations as are not conformable to theſe principles muſt be imputed to the difficulty of pronouncing many of the Shanſcrit combinations of letters, or to the indolent habits of the moderns.

S

Such

Such for inftance as দেখন *to fee*, from দর্শন° বেঁকন *to bend* (intrans:) from বঙ্কন° &c. Thefe verbs alone would fill a copious vocabulary.

I have not inferted fuch words as have not been applied in the feveral moods and tenfes of verbs, by fome or other of the antient authors. Shanfcrit muft formerly have been much more current in Bengal than we now find it, or the more learned Bramins muft not at that time have thought it infinitely beneath their dignity to compile books in the ভাসা or language of difcourfe. There are a thoufand terms which have the form of infinitives, and are derived from Shanfcrit roots, but which have not once ferved in the capacity of verbs. If ever the Bengalefe fhould acquire a knowledge of the liberal fciences, and a tafte for refined compofitions, this unappropriated ftock will afford equal refources to the Poet and the Philofopher. It is a mine which in fkillful hands would well repay the trouble of working.

In the Shanfcrit language as in the Greek, there are forms of infinitives and of participles comprehenfive of time ; there are alfo other branches of the verb, that feem to refemble the gerunds and fupines of the Latin. All thefe modifications of the verb, together with nouns of agency, and every other derivative from a Dhaat, (which is not characterifed by one or other

of

of the temporal inflexions) are arranged by the Shanſcrit grammarians in a ſeparate chapter, immediately following that of
verbs.

কৃৎ is the general name for all the terminations by which
theſe ſeveral forms are diſtinguiſhed; and the claſs itſelf is for
this reaſon denominated কৃদন্ত or words ending with a কৃৎ

The number of theſe terminations, including thoſe which
on account of the different letters that occur at the end of the
Dhaat, have two or more proviſional forms to the ſame meaning, may amount to about one hundred; and therefore a Shanſcrit verb muſt ſupply a variety of derivatives at leaſt as copious
as thoſe of the Greek: and ſome terms I think I have met
with, whoſe meaning could not be fully rendered by a ſingle
word in any other language.

But as the ſcope of my work does not admit of a diſtinĉt chapter for the কৃদন্ত claſs, and as an explanation of them is by
no means neceſſary for the underſtanding of the Bengal language, it will ſuffice to have here given a general idea of the
manner in which this part of the ſcience of grammar has been
treated by the Bramins. I ſhall therefore confine myſelf to a
ſpecies of কৃদন্ত (if I may be allowed to borrow the expreſſion) which belongs to the Bengal idiom only.

The

The form which I would defcribe, is a noun of reciproca-
tion, implying either a mutual co-operation or a mutual oppofi-
tion. This noun is compofed of the participle of the paffive
voice prefixed to the participle prefent of the active: as of the
verb হনন *to wound* হান| is the paffive participle *wounded*,
and হানি the active participle *wounding*. Thefe two united
make হানাহানি *a mutual wounding* ; as

দুই বীরে হানাহানি সংগ্রাম ভিতরে

" There was *a mutual wounding* by the two heroes in the midft
" of the battle."

Upon the fame principle are formed the following words and
many others.

কাটাকাটি	from কাটন	to cut.
ধরাধরি	from ধরন	to feize.
মারামারি	from মারন	to beat.
দেখাদেখি	from দেখন	to behold.
ডাকাডাকি	from ডাকন	to call.
মিষামিষি	from মিষন	to mingle.
জড়াজড়ি	from জড়ন	to wreftle.

জড়াজড়ি করি দুহে পড়ে ভুমিতলে

" The two warriors *wreftling with each other* fell to the ground.'

This

This kind of alliterative found is particularly pleafing to a Bengal ear; for which reafon a great number of words has been formed in imitation of this fpecies, which preferve their reciprocative energy, tho' derived from common nouns. Such are কানাকানি *with ear to ear*, (that is *a mutual whifpering*) from কান *an ear.*

মুখামুখি *face to face*,   from মুখ *the face.*

গলাগলি *a mutual embracing*,   from গলা *the neck.*

চুলাচুলি *a mutual plucking of the hair*,   from চুল *the hair.*

দেশাদেশি *a mutual inhabiting of the fame kingdom.*

বনাবনি *a mutual exertion of ftrength.*

Some few words of this fort feem to imply completion; as

মাসামাসি *a complete month.*   বেনাবেনি *a complete day.*

তরাতরি *complete hafte.*

A third clafs, which may be referred to this fpecies, confifts of words contrived to imitate certain founds, by the reiteration of particular letters or fyllables. Thefe have not the letter আ inferted in the middle, and do not convey any mutual or reciprocative meaning.

থরথরি *a noife like that of trees in a ftorm.*

ঝরঝরি *a noife like the dafhing of waves.*

ঝনঝন *a noife like the falling of a fhower.*

চনচন a noiſe like the tinkling of bells.

হড়হড়ি a noiſe like the rattling of **carriages.**

ছড়ছড়ি a loud noiſe as of guns.

মক্মকি a croaking like that of frogs.

Example.

ঝরঝরি জলের বাওর থড়থড়ি ।
দুই জনে সুইয়া থাকিব গলাধরি ॥

" There is the daſhing of the water, and the whiſtling of **the**
" breeze ;

" I will enfold you in my arms and we will ſleep together."

And theſe terms are often further diſtinguiſhed by the word

শব্দ which in its more enlarged ſenſe ſignifies noiſe in general; **as**

অবিশ্রান্ত পড়ে চোট করে হানাহানি ।
ঝনঝন চনচন শব্দ মাত্র সুনি ॥

" Wounds fall without ceaſing, and inflict reciprocal gaſhes,
" I hear only the din and claſhing ſound of the battle."

Sometimes a noun is repeated in the oblique caſe either with
a reciprocative idea, or to gratify the taſte for alliteration ; **as**

মনেমনে with a hearty good will, or ſpontaneouſly,
from মন the heart.

দন্তেদন্তে with tooth to tooth.

অন্যোঅন্যে one another.

ঘরেঘেরে from houſe to houſe &c.

মনেমনে মহা রাজা করেন বিচার

" The Maahaa Raajaa of his own accord makes inveſtigation. "

দুই হস্তী মিষামিষি দন্তেদন্তে কষাকষি
ক্ষ্ত্রবান পাণ্ডুর নন্দন

" The two elephants were mingled in the confliᴄt, with tooth
" againſt tooth, ſtruggling with each other; and the ſon of
" Paandoo trembled."

অন্যোঅন্যে সারথী কাটিন অস্ত্র রথ

" The charioteers hacked one another's horſes and carriage."

CHAPTER V.

OF ATTRIBUTES AND RELATIONS.

ALL the terms which ſerve to qualify, to diſtinguiſh, or
to augment either *ſubſtance* or *aᴄtion*, are claſſed by the
Shanſcrit grammarians under the head of বিশেষন which literally ſignifies *increaſe* or *addition*. According to their arrangement, a ſimple ſentence conſiſts of three members, কর্ত্তা *the*
agent,

agent, ক্রিয়া *the action* and কর্ম্ম *the subject* : which in a grammatical sense are reduced to two : শব্দ the *noun,* (whether a-
gent or subject) and ক্রিয়া the *verb.* All such words as tend
to specificate or to amplify the noun, are denominated শব্দ
বিশেষন which we may construe *adjectives* or *epithets;* and
such as are applied to denote relation or connection are called
শব্দযোগ or connectives of nouns, and by European grammarians are styled *prepositions.*

Those particles which in any manner affect the verb, have
the name of ক্রিয়াবিশেষন or *attributes of verbs.*

In this chapter therefore I shall include all the terms which
relate to either of these divisions; and shall class them under
their respective heads : শব্দবিশেষন and শব্দযোগ will
then rank together as attributes of nouns, and the ক্রিয়া
বিশেষন will be made to comprise conjunctions as well
as adverbs : because the former are employed to denote the relations of tenses, in the same manner as prepositions are to mark
those of nouns; and therefore properly belong to verbs, which
are the hinges of every sentence.

Thus I hope I shall be found to comprehend all the parts of
speech, as generally distinguished, without paying a servile attention

tion to the received fyftem of grammatical arrangements.

শব্দবিশেষন or the fimple adjective of the Bengalefe, has
no variation of gender, cafe or number. In this refpect it perfectly refembles the idiom of the Englifh; for as we ufe the
word *great* indifcriminately to a mafculine or feminine noun; fo
the Bengalefe fay মহারাজা a *great* prince, and মহারানী
a *great* princefs: So আইবড় an adjective with a mafculine
termination is applied to a feminine. Example.

এক পুত্রী আইবড় বিদ্যা নাম তার

" He has one daughter *unmarried*, her name is B*eedyaa* "

Neither is the adjective fubject to inflexion; but the fign of
the cafe is confined to the fubftantive with which it agrees; as

মহা নাদে রোদন করয়ে সৈন্য গন

" The troops lamented with *a mighty noife.* "

So alfo its form is confined to the fingular number, even
when joined to a plural noun; as

সকল পণ্ডিতগন হইল পরাজয়

" *All the Pundits* were overcome. "

But thofe derivative attributes, which are alternately adjectives
and concrete nouns, generally preferve the diftictions of gender
which they all poffefs in the Shanfcrit.

T

Here

Here therefore I fhall endeavour to give a concife defcription of the feveral forms of adjectives with their derivation, as far as they ufually occur in the Bengal language.

1. Verbal concretes, or participles of agency immediately formed from Shanfcrit roots, have the termination তা for the mafculine, and ত্রী for the feminine.

Mafculine.		Feminine.		
কর্তা	*an agent.*	কর্ত্রী	from	কৃ
দাতা	*a giver.*	দাত্রী	from	দা

2. Mafculines ending in আ and আন derived from crude nouns in ন and ए have their feminine termination in অতী

Mafculine.		Feminine.		
যুবা	*a young man, (juvenis)*	যুবতী	from	যুবন
শ্রীমন	*rich,*	শ্রীমতী	from	শ্রীমৎ

কোন অভিলাসে বিরহ বাতাসে জানাইনা যুবতী

" How eagerly didft thou enflame the *young girl* with the breath " of perfidy ! "

3. Concretes are made from abftract terms by adding ঈ for the mafculine, and ইনী for the feminine ; as

Maculine.		Feminine.			
পাপী	*criminal.*	পাপিনী	from	পাপ	*a crime.*
দুঃখী	*miferable.*	দুঃখিনী	from	দুঃখ	*mifery.*

জনমদুখিনী মোরে করিলেক বিধি

" God hath made me *miserable from my birth.*" (spoken by a woman)

The same form is applied to local possessives; as বঙ্গানী *a man of Bengal* বঙ্গালিনী *a woman of Bengal* &c.

4. When the masculine ends with a consonant, or ই short, the feminine termination is ঈ long; as

Masculine.		Feminine.
সতি	*constant.*	সতী
সুমুথ	*beautiful.*	সুমুথী

Example.

সীতা গো পরম সতী তার শুন দুর্গতি

" O woman! Seetaa was very *constant.* Hear her unfortunate " story."

Adjectives and concrete nouns implying cause, possession, plenty &c. assume the terminations কার অঙ্কর বান বৎ and বন্ত· মান মন্ত ধর and ধাম as

ধুম্বুকার *smoak-making,* from ধুম্ব *smoak.*
ভয়ঙ্কর *causing fear,* from ভয় *fear.*

ধুম্বকার ধুম্বু করি কিন অন্ধকার

" The smoak-maker, producing a smoak, caused a compleat " darkness."

পুন্যবান	*holy,*	from	পুন্য	*holiness.*
বনবৎ & বনবন্ত	*strong,*	from	বন	*strength.*
বুদ্ধিমান	*wise,*	from	বুদ্ধি	*wisdom.*
ভাগ্যমন্ত	*fortunate,*	from	ভাগ্য	*prosperity*

জাহার ঘরে সদাবাস নক্ষ্মী আর অনন্ত ।
সেই জন পুন্যবান বড় ভাগ্যমব ॥

" In the house of whomsoever *Lokhmee* and *Ononto* constantly
[reside,
" That man is *holy* and most *fortunate*."

ভাগ্যধর	*prosperous.*	from	ভাগ্য	*prosperity.*
গুনধাম	*intelligent,*	from	গুন	*knowledge.*

রাজা বড় ভাগ্যধর কাছে নদী দামোদর

" The *Raajaa* is most *prosperous* ; near him is the river *Daamodor*."

5. The negative particles অ নি নির and বি prefixed to words form adjectives of privation ; as

অচল	*motionless,*	from	চলন	*to go.*
অমৃত	*immortal,*	from	মৃত	*to die.*
অপূর্ব্ব	*unprecedented,*	from	পূর্ব্ব	*before.*
অসক্ত	*weak,*	from	সক্ত	*strong.*

অপূর্ব্ব করিব বুহ অদ্ভুত মানুষে

" I will conſtruct an *unprecedented* caſtle, wonderful among
" men."

নিপাত	*leafleſs,*	from	পাত	*a leaf.*
নিধন	*poor, (inops)*	from	ধন	*wealth.*
নিরস্ত্র	*unarmed,*	from	অস্ত্র	*a weapon.*
নির্ভয়	*fearleſs,*	from	ভয়	*fear.*

দুহে হইন নিরস্ত্র করিয়া মহা রন

" The Heroes were both without weapons, having ſupported a
" mighty conflict. "

| বিসম | *incomparable,* | from | সম | *like.* |
| বিয়োগী | *widowed,* | from | যোগ | *union.* |

আসাড়ে নবিন মেঘ গভির গর্জ্জন ৷
বিয়োগীর যমসম সংযোগীর প্রান ৷৷

" In the month Aaaſaar the new cloud makes a deep bellowing ;
" To the widow like the miniſter of death, but life to the wife."

6. An elegant claſs of compound attributes is produced by
the junction of a ſubſtantive and an adjective, or of two ſubſtantives.; as

মৃগাক্ষ *ſtag-eyed,* from মৃগ *a ſtag,* and অক্ষ *an eye.*

নির্ভয়হৃদয় *of an undaunted breaſt.*

মহামতি or মহামনি *of a great heart.*

ক্রোধমন *of an angry disposition.*

হরিস অন্তর *of an agreeable humour.*

দুরাচার *wicked,* from দুর *distant,* and আচার *an institute of religion.*

ব্রাহ্মনের অমান্য করিস দুরাচার ৷
আজি আমি ইহার করিব প্রতিকার ॥

" Dost thou dishonour the Bramin, O *wicked wretch*!

" I will to day make an ample reparation for it."

মৃতরূপা having the appearance of death, from মৃত *death,* and রূপ *figure.*

গুনসাগর *learned,* (litterally, a fea of learning) from গুন *fcience,* and সাগর *the ocean.*

অধোমুখ with a down caft countenance, from অধো *down,* and মুখ *the face.*

আকার fignifying *figure* or *appearance* is frequently added to an adjective or fubftantive to form a compound epithet of fimilitude ; as

মানুষাকার *like a man.*

সুক্লাকার *of a white appearance.*

রক্তাকার *like blood,* &c.

7. The terminations তর and তম form the comparative and ſuperlative degrees of Shanſcrit adjectives; as মন্দ *bad*, মন্দতর *worſe*, মন্দতম *worſt*. দূর *diſtant*, দূরতর *more diſtant*, দূরতম *moſt diſtant*.

But the latter of theſe inflexions is never uſed by the Bengaleſe; and the former very ſparingly; and always in a ſenſe that might perhaps rather be termed an indefinite augmentation, than a compariſon; Thus

আনন্দিত বৃকোদর যুদ্ধ করে ঘোরতর

" Brokodor elated fights *more fiercely*."

The definitive compariſon is expreſſed by a ſimple adjective, both in the Bengaleſe and Hindoſtanic idioms: And the inferior ſubject is diſtinguiſhed by a particle anſvvering to *than*; as

সুগ্রীব হইতে বালী রাজা অতি মহা বীর ৷
রঘুনাথের বানে তেহ হইল অস্থির ॥

" Baalee Raajaa was a much greater hero *than* Soogreeb,
" Yet even he was put to flight by the weapons of Roghoonaath."

Attributes of augmentation may be prefixed to all ſimple adjectives, to enlarge or extend their power; ſuch are বড় *great* পরম *very*, বহুত *much* or *many*, অতি *much*, &c. as বড় সুন্দর *very fair*, অতি অনুপাম *extremely beautiful*, পরমসতী *remarkably conſtant*.

Example.

বড় সুন্দর সেই অতি অনুপাম ।
সুনিনাম বিদ্যার পতি অতি গুনধাম ॥

" This perſon *very* fair and *extremely* beautiful,

" I have heard to be the *moſt* accompliſhed huſband of *Beedyaa*."

অতি is prefixed to the comparative degree to form a ſuperlative ; as

রথ চালাইয়া দেহ অতি সিঘ্নুতর

" Cauſe the chariot to come hither *moſt* expeditiouſly. "

Adjectives are frequently doubled to augment their meaning as বড় বড় *very large,* ছোট ছোট *very ſmall.*

Example.

ছোট বড়সিতে মারে বড় বড় মিন ।
প্রানে না মারে তবু মুথে রাথে চিন ॥

" With a ſmall hook he ſtrikes a *very large* fiſh ;

" It does not affect his life, yet imprints a mark in his mouth."

The particle সম prefixed to a word, makes a kind of ſuperlative ; as পূর্ন *full,* সম্পূর্ন *very full.*

The ſame particle ſubjoined, is a contraction of সমান and like it denotes ſimilitude or reſemblance ; as

তোমাসম যোদ্ধাপতি নাহিক আমার

" We

" We have no warrior *like* yourfelf. "

মেঘের বিক্রমসম মাঘের হিমানি

" The cold of the month Maagh is *like* the ftrength of the

" cloud. "

মহাভারতের কথা অমৃত সমান ৷

কাসীরাম দাস কহে শুন পুন্যবান ॥

" The words of the Mohaabhaarot, *equal to immortality*

" Kaafeeraam Daas utters; hear them O ye righteous ! "

So alfo are ufed তুল and তুল্য from the Shanfcrit infini-

tive তুনন° *to weigh*; as

বেদ তুল্য জানি আমি তোমার বচন

" I confider your counfel as *equally weighty* with the Bades. "

Under the clafs of *Attributes to nouns*, I comprehend শব্দ

যোগ or *Prepofitions*. They are fubftitutes for cafes, which

could not have been extended to the number neceffary for ex-

preffing all the feveral relations and predicaments in which a

noun may ftand, without caufing too much embarraffment in

the form of a declenfion.

Moft of the particles applied in this capacity are nouns ex-

preffive of fituation, order, connexion, or fome other relation;

and as they have generally a reference to *place*, are indifferently

U   ufed

uſed in the nominative, and in the ſeventh caſe with the locative termination এ   as ওপর or ওপরে *above*, ভিতর
or ভিতরে *within*, &c.

But to diſtinguiſh the শব্দযোগ or words having only a
relative ſignification, from the principal ſubſtantives to which
they relate, it is neceſſary to obſerve that the noun *in regimine*
with a prepoſition ſhould properly be in the poſſeſſive caſe, and
prior in poſition ; as they ſay পৃথিবীর মধ্যে *in the midſt of*
the world, but never মধ্যে পৃথিবীর becauſe the world is the
containing ſubject ; and মধ্যে ſerves only to mark the nature
of the connexion, which ſubſiſts between the world and ſome
other ſubject ; as

পৃথিবীর মধ্যে কেবা নাজানে তোমারে

" Who *in the world* (i.e. of thoſe perſons contained in the world)
" is unacquainted with you ? "

The moſt common of the শব্দযোগ are theſe which follow.
ভিতর *within*, মধ্যে মাঝে *in the midſt of* ; (anſwer to
the ſeventh, or locative caſe) সহ সহিত সঙ্গে *with*,
together with, হইতে *by* ; (the third Shanſcrit caſe) as

কৃষ্ণ হইতে গড়া হইয়াছিল এই ঘর

" This houſe was erected *by* Kreeſhno. "

হইতে *from* ; (the fifth caſe) as

হেন কালে সাত্যকি ঐচিল ভূমি হইতে

" At that inftant Saatyokee arofe *from* the ground. "

বিনা বিনে or বিনু *without*. (*fine*)

বাহির *without*, on the outfide. (*extra*) Example.

মেঘের বিক্রম সম মাঘের হিমালি ।
ঘরের বাহির নহে যেই যুবা বলি ॥

" The cold of the month Maagh is like the ftrength of the cloud ;

" Then I fay the youth fhould not be *without* the houfe. "

আগে *before*, either in time or place.

কারন বিষয় হেতু *on account of.*

দিগে *towards.* তরে *inftead of.* তলে নাম or নাব

below, beneath, down. ঊপর *above, upon.* নিকট স্থান

near; to, at. (*apud*)

স্থান is a very difficult word. It properly fignifies *place*, (ftatio) and is derived from the dhaat স্থা which anfwers to *fto* ; as in Virgil.

" Dum *ftabat* regno incolumis —— " i.e. While he *remained* fecure in his kingdom.

But স্থান muft generally be conftrued *to* or *from* in Englifh ; as

এক নিবেদন আমি করি তোর স্থান

" I make one requeft *to you.* " [apud te]

স্থির স্থানে সোমদত্ত পাইয়া এই বর

" Somdott having obtained this favour *from* God," [apud Deum]

স্থির is derived from the fame root, and fignifies *ftabilis, immotus,* fo that স্থির স্থান means *apud immobile numen.*

The word স্থান feems in very early times to have been adopted by the Perfians, who formed of it an infeparable particle of *place*; as ـگلستان *a bed of rofes*, ـهندوستان *India*, literally, a country of fwarthy people.

The doctrine of derivatives from one language to another has been fo much abufed by fanciful and unwarrantable inftances, drawn from the meer refemblance of founds, that every hint now ftarted on the fubject is defpifed as frivolous, or fufpected as fallacious. If I might venture to propofe a rule in fuch cafes, it fhould be this ;

Whenever in a compound word we find one or more of the component fyllables, which are entire words, having a precife and feparate meaning in fome other language, tho' not in that where the compound term is ufed, we need not fcruple to pronounce the original dialect to be that from whence the fignificant fyllables proceed ; as in the prefent inftance, where ستان taken by itfelf as a Perfian word, conveys no idea what-

ever,

ever, but when joined to other words, denotes place or fituation. স্থান in Shanſcrit actually fignifies *a place* or *ſtation*, and
is itſelf derived from a primary root of the ſame language.

But if a ſimple term be found to exiſt in two languages, and
to have the ſame fignification in each, I would then enquire
whether that word be not derived, in one of them, from ſome
general term or root; and wherever ſuch root were found, I
would pronounce that language to be the original : thus *ſerpens*
a ſerpent comes from *ſerpo*. but I do not doubt that the latter
owes its derivation to সর্প the Shanſcrit word for a ſerpent,
which ſprings from the dhaat সৃপ a general term for *gliding
motion.*

Let me here curſorily obſerve, that as the Latin is an earlier dialect than the Greek. as we now have it, ſo it bears much
more reſemblance to the Shanſcrit, both in words, inflexions
and terminations.

ক্রিয়া বিশেষন Adverbs require no deſcription or remark.

Adverbs of time.

এথন now.	তথন or ততক্ষন then.
কদাচ ever.	কদাচন never.
কথন at any time.	যথন whenſoever.
এথনতক or এই পর্য্যন্ত yet.	

পুনরপি once more.

ইহার পর afterwards.

সদা সর্ব্বদা always.

ফের again.

আজি to day.

কল্য to morrow, or yesterday.

পরসু the day after to morrow, or the day before yesterday.

তরসু two days hence.

দিনে by day.

রাত্রে রজনীতে by night.

প্রভাতে in the morning.

বৈকালে in the afternoon.

পূর্ব্ব আগে before.

পশ্চাৎ পাছে after, since.

Adverbs of place.

এথানে here.

ওথানে there.

হের hither.

হোর thither.

কোথা কোথায় whither.

স্থানেস্থানে in different places

নিকট nigh.

দূর far off.

ফের back, (rursus) from

ফেরন to turn.

ইতি *thus far*, the formulary at the conclusion of a book, or writing.

Adverbs of specification &c.

কেন why?

কি কেমন what? how?

অতি very.

প্রায় almost.

কিছু scarcely.

এব° particularly.

বিস্তারিত videlicet. নিশ্চয় অবস্য certainly. না not.

All indeclinable adjectives may be ufed adverbially in Bengalefe, as the neuter gender of adjectives in Greek and Latin.

Conjunctions.

ও and.

আর alfo, moreover.

যদি if, although, when.

কিন্তু but, yet, neverthelefs.

কি কিবা কিয়া or.

অতয়েব therefore.

তভু তমু notwithftanding.

যাবত while. তাবত fo long.

যাবত কল্পেতে আমার রহে প্রান ৷

তাবত পূজিব আমি দেব ভগবান ॥

" *While* life remains in my body,

" *So long* will I worfhip the Deity Bhogowaan."

CHAPTER. VI.

Of Numbers.

THE learned feem no longer to doubt, that the ufe of numerical figures was firft derived from India: and indeed the antiquity of their application in that country far exceeds the powers of inveftigation.

The denominations of the cardinal numbers are fo irregular

in

in Bengalefe, that I find it will be neceffary to exhibit them as far as one hundred. And it muft be obferved as a particularity, that the ninth numeral of every feries of ten, is not fpecified by the term of nine in the common order of progreffion, but takes its appellation from the feries immediately above; as for inftance the number *twenty nine* is not expreffed by *nobeefh*, which fhould feem the proper denomination, but is called *oonteefh*, or one lefs than thirty. So *thirty nine* is *oonchaaleefh* or one lefs than forty.

All the numerals in Shanfcrit have different forms for the different genders, as in Arabic; but are invariable in Bengalefe.

Bengalefe.		Shanfcrit.	
১	এক	একঃ	one.
২	দুই	দ্রৌ	two.
৩	তিন	ত্রয়ঃ	three.
৪	চারি	চত্বারঃ	four.
৫	পাঁচ	পঞ্চ	five.
৬	ছয়	ষট্‌	fix.
৭	সাত	সপ্ত	feven.
৮	আট	অষ্ট	eight.
৯	নয়	নবাঃ	nine.

১০	দশ	দশ	ten.
১১	এগার	একাদশ	eleven.
১২	বার	দ্বাদশ	twelve.
১৩	তের	ত্রয়োদশ	thirteen.
১৪	চৌদ্দ	চতুর্দশ	fourteen.
১৫	পোনের	পঞ্চদশ	fifteen.
১৬	ষোল	ষোড়শ	sixteen.
১৭	সতের	সপ্তদশ	seventeen.
১৮	আটার	অষ্টাদশ	eighteen.
১৯	ঙনিশ	ঙনবিংশতিঃ	nineteen.
২০	বিশ	বিংশতি	twenty.
২১	এক্দশ	একবিংশতিঃ	twenty one.
২২	বাইশ	দ্বিবিংশতিঃ	twenty two.
২৩	তেইশ	ত্রয়োবিংশতিঃ	twenty three.
২৪	চব্বিশ	চতুর্বিংশতিঃ	twenty four.
২৫	পঁচিশ	পঞ্চবিংশতিঃ	twenty five.
২৬	ছাব্বিশ	ষড়িবংশতিঃ	twenty six.
২৭	সাতাইশ	সপ্তবিংশতিঃ	twenty seven.
২৮	আটাইশ	অষ্টাবিংশতিঃ	twenty eight.
২৯	ঙনত্রিশ	ঙনত্রিংশৎ	twenty nine.
৩০	ত্রিশ	ত্রিংশৎ	thirty.

V

৩১	একত্রিশ	একত্রিংশৎ	thirty one.
৩২	বত্তিশ	দ্বাত্রিংশৎ	thirty two.
৩৩	তেত্রিশ	ত্রয়স্ত্রিংশৎ	thirty three.
৩৪	চৌতিশ	চতুস্ত্রিংশৎ	thirty four.
৩৫	পঁইতিশ	পঞ্চত্রিংশৎ	thirty five.
৩৬	ছত্তিশ	ষট্‌ত্রিংশৎ	thirty fix.
৩৭	সাঁইতিশ	সপ্তত্রিংশৎ	thirty seven.
৩৮	আটতিশ	অষ্টত্রিংশৎ	thirty eight.
৩৯	ঊনচল্লিশ	নবত্রিংশৎ	thirty nine.
৪০	চল্লিশ	চত্বারিংশৎ	forty.
৪১	একচল্লিশ	একচত্বারিংশৎ	forty one.
৪২	ব্যাল্লিশ	দ্বিচত্বারিংশৎ	forty two.
৪৩	তেতাল্লিশ	ত্রিচত্বারিংশৎ	forty three.
৪৪	চৌয়াল্লিশ	চতুশ্চত্বারিংশৎ	forty four.
৪৫	পঁয়তাল্লিশ	পঞ্চচত্বারিংশৎ	forty five.
৪৬	ছেচল্লিশ	ষট্‌চত্বারিংশৎ	forty fix.
৪৭	সাতচল্লিশ	সপ্তচত্বারিংশৎ	forty seven.
৪৮	আটচল্লিশ	অষ্টচত্বারিংশৎ	forty eight.
৪৯	ঊনপঞ্চাশ	একোনপঞ্চাশৎ	forty nine.
৫০	পঞ্চাশ	পঞ্চাশৎ	fifty.
৫১	একান্ন	একপঞ্চাশৎ	fifty one.
৫২	বায়ান্ন	দ্বিপঞ্চাশৎ	fifty two.

৫৩	ত্রিপ্যান্	ত্রিপঞ্চাশৎ	fifty three.
৫৪	চৌয়ান্	চতুঃপঞ্চাশৎ	fifty four.
৫৫	পঞ্চান্	পঞ্চপঞ্চাশৎ	fifty five.
৫৬	ছাপ্পান্	ষট্পঞ্চাশৎ	fifty fix.
৫৭	সাতান্	সপ্তপঞ্চাশৎ	fifty feven.
৫৮	আটান্	অষ্টপঞ্চাশৎ	fifty eight.
৫৯	ঊনষাটি	একোনষষ্টিঃ	fifty nine.
৬০	ষাটি	ষষ্টি	fixty.
৬১	একষট্টি	একষষ্টিঃ	fixty one.
৬২	বাষট্টি	দ্বিষষ্টিঃ	fixty two.
৬৩	তেষট্টি	ত্রিষষ্টিঃ	fixty three.
৬৪	চৌষট্টি	চতুঃষষ্টিঃ	fixty four.
৬৫	পঁয়ষট্টি	পঞ্চষষ্টিঃ	fixty five.
৬৬	ছষট্টি	ষট্ষষ্টিঃ	fixty fix.
৬৭	সাতষট্টি	সপ্তষষ্টিঃ	fixty feven.
৬৮	আটষট্টি	অষ্টষষ্টিঃ	fixty eight.
৬৯	ঊনষত্তোর	একোনসপ্ততি॰	fixty nine.
৭০	সত্তোর	সপ্ততিঃ	feventy.
৭১	একাত্তোর	একসপ্ততিঃ	feventy one.
৭২	বাহাত্তোর	দ্বিসপ্ততিঃ	feventy two.
৭৩	তেহাত্তোর	ত্রিসপ্ততিঃ	feventy three.
৭৪	চৌহাত্তোর	চতুঃসপ্ততিঃ	feventy four.

৭৫	পঁচাত্তোর	পঞ্চসপ্ততিঃ	seventy five.
৭৬	ছেয়াত্তোর	সটষপ্ততিঃ	seventy six.
৭৭	সাতাত্তোর	সপ্তসপ্ততিঃ	seventy seven.
৭৮	আটাত্তোর	অষ্টসপ্ততিঃ	seventy eight.
৭৯	ঊনআশি	নবসপ্ততিঃ	seventy nine.
৮০	আশি	অশীতিঃ	eighty.
৮১	একাশি	একাশীতিঃ	eighty one.
৮২	বিরাশি	দ্বাশীতিঃ	eighty two.
৮৩	তিরাশি	ত্র্যশীতিঃ	eighty three.
৮৪	চৌরাশি	চতুরশীতিঃ	eighty four.
৮৫	পঁচাশি	পঞ্চাশীতিঃ	eighty five.
৮৬	ছেয়াশি	ষড়শীতিঃ	eighty six.
৮৭	সাতাশি	সপ্তাশীতিঃ	eighty seven.
৮৮	আঠাশি	অষ্টাশীতিঃ	eighty eight.
৮৯	ঊননয়ি	একোননবতিঃ	eighty nine.
৯০	নয়ি	নবতিঃ	ninety.
৯১	একানয়ি	একনবতিঃ	ninety one.
৯২	বিরানয়ি	দ্বিনবতিঃ	ninety two.
৯৩	তিরানয়ি	ত্রিনবতিঃ	ninety three.
৯৪	চৌরানয়ি	চতুর্নবতিঃ	ninety four.
৯৫	পঁচানয়ি	পঞ্চনবতিঃ	ninety five.
৯৬	ছেয়ানয়ি	ষন্নবতিঃ	ninety six.

৯৭	সাতানয়ি	সপ্তনবতিঃ	ninety feven.
৯৮	আঠানয়ি	অষ্টনবতিঃ	ninety eight.
৯৯	নিরানয়ি	নবনবতিঃ	ninety nine.
১০০	শতঃ	শ	one hundred.

Ordinal Numbers.

Bengalefe.	Shanfcrit.	
একত্রি · পয়লা	পৃথম	firft.
দোয়জা · দোষরা	দ্বিতীয়	fecond.
তেয়জা · তেষরা	ত্রিতীয়	third.
চৌঠা	চতুর্থ	fourth.
পাঁচত্রি	পঞ্চম	fifth.
ছয়ত্রি	ষষ্ট	fixth.
সাতত্রি	সপ্তম	feventh.
আটত্রি	অষ্টম	eighth.
নয়ত্রি	নবম	ninth.
দশত্রি	দশম	tenth.
এগারত্রি	একাদশ	eleventh.
বারত্রি	দ্বাদশ	twelfth.
তেরত্রি	ত্রয়োদশ	thirteenth.
চৌঢত্রি	চতুর্দশ	fourteenth.
পোনেরত্রি	পঞ্চদশ	fifteenth.

যোনক্ত্রি	যোড়শ	sixteenth.
সতেরক্ত্রি	সপ্তদশ	seventeenth.
আচারক্ত্রি	অষ্টাদশ	eighteenth.
ওনিশা	ঔনবিৎশতি	nineteenth.
বিশা · বিশক্ত্রি	বিৎশ	twentieth.

From hence the Ordinals are all formed by adding আ to the cardinals.

Of the Bengal Arithmetic.

As the numerical figures of India are certainly the prototype of those now used in Europe, it is probable that the simpler rules at least of Arithmetic are derived from the same source: for other nations of the East have invented different processes for arriving at the same conclusions. Thus the Chinese perform all their computations by means of a sett of Beads; and the Persians use a species of figures which are in fact Arabic words; and add up the most confiderable sums, without being in the least affisted by the position of units under ¹ units, tens under tens &c. Perhaps there may yet exist other modes of arithmetic of which we have no notion; so that the strict conformity in the arrangement and application of figures, as well as

in

in their forms,   which we find between Hindoſtan and Europe, ſhould not raſhly be imputed to chance.

The Bengaleſe in all their accompts make particular uſe of the number *four*.   Their Bankers always count the largeſt ſums of money by diviſions of *fours*, and the computations of numbers of all other things are always made in the ſame manner: and upon all occaſions *four* is their grand multiple and diviſor. This is probably a veſtige of the moſt original and antient airthmetic, when invention had proceeded no farther than to number the fingers, and then repeat the ſame proceſs.

Even to this day the Bengaleſe reckon by the joints of their fingers, beginning with the lower joint of the little finger and proceeding to the thumb, the ball of which is alſo included as a joint; and thus the whole hand contains *fifteen*.

From this method of performing numeration on the joints, ariſes that well-known cuſtom among the Indian merchants, of ſettling all matters of purchaſe and ſale by joining their hands beneath a cloth, and then touching the different joints as they would increaſe or diminiſh their demands.

As a proof how far ſome branches of Science have been cnltivated in India, I ſhall here give a ſpecimen of the prodigious extent of the Shanſcrit numeration by diſtinct terms.

এক°	. . .	১	One.
দশ°	. . .	০.	Ten.
শত°	. . .	০	a Hundred.
সহস্র°	. . .	০	a Thousand.
অযুত°	. . .	০	X. Thousands.
লক্ষ°	. . .	০	C. Thousands.
নিযুত°	. . .	০	a Million.
কোটিঃ	. . .	০	X. Millions.
অর্বুদ	. . .	০	C. Millions.
মহা অর্বুদ	. .	০	a Thousand Millions.
পদ্ম	. . .	০	X. Thousand Millions.
মহা পদ্ম	. .	০	C. Thousand Millions.
থর্ব্ব	. . .	০	a Billion.
মহা থর্ব্ব	. .	০	X. Billions.
শঙ্খ	. . .	০	C. Billions.
মহাশঙ্খ	. .	০	a Thousand Billions.
হাহা	. . .	০	X. Thousand Billions.
মহা হাহা	. .	০	C. Thousand Billions.
ধুন	. . .	০	a Trillion.
মহা ধুন	. .	০	X. Trillions.
অক্ষৌহিনী	. .	০	C. Trillions.
মহা অক্ষৌহিনী		০	a Thousand Trillions.

The conftituent parts of accounts, and fome arithmetical Tables.

চৌটি	a quarter of any thing indifcriminately.
সিকি	a quarter of money.
পোয়া	a quarter of weights and meafures.
আধা	a half of any thing.
আধিনি	a half of money.
অর্দ্ধেক	a half of meafures.
তিনপোয়া	three quarters of any thing.
সওয়া	one and a quarter.
ডেড়	one and a half.
পৌনে দুই	one and three quarters.
সওয়াদুই	two and a quarter.
আড়াই	two and a half.
পৌনেতিন	two and three quarters.
সওয়াতিন	three and a quarter.
সাডেতিন	three and a half.
পৌনেচারি	three and three quarters.

The fractions are denominated in the fame manner, joined to all larger fums or quantities.

W

The

The reader is not to be told that the shells called *Cowries* are current in Bengal, as the lowest species of money : They are upon on average in the proportion of five thousand to the rupee.

Bengal accounts are divided into পাকা and কাঁচা which litterally signify *ripe*, and *unripe*.   An unripe, or kaachaa account is when the highest denomination in the line of addition is the কাহন kaahon,   or some what more than a quarter of a rupee : viz. such accounts as are used by the petty retailers in the Bazar, wherein no single article amounts to one rupee.

The paakaa, or ripe account is when the rupee is the highest denomination, or standard unit in the line of addition ; and each of the subordinate fractional figures is increased in value proportionably to the increase of the standard unit from the kaahon to the rupee ; which proportion is regulated by the price of cowries in the Bazar.   But in the paakaa and in the kaachaa accounts, the same figures,   both for the units and fractions, hold the same arithmetical places.   To shew therefore that an account is kaachaa, the word কড়ি is written at top, as we write *L. S. D.*   to denote the paakaa account the word কপোয়া or তঙ্ক is superscribed in the same manner.

Gross commodities of all kinds are sold by the সের far, a weight nearly answering to two pounds avoirdupoise, and of which 40 make মন a maund.   The

The Sar is divided into পোয়া or quarters, and thofe again are fubdivided into ছটাক of which four make a পোয়া

Precious metals and jewels are weighed by the তোলা the মাসা and the রতি. তোলা tolaa is derived from the word তুলন *to weigh*, and therefore fignifies a ftandard, or precife weight by which all others may be regulated. It is alfo the mean weight between precious and grofs articles, as it is the higheft denomination of the former, and the loweft of the latter. The ficca rupee, properly called টাকা taakaa in Bengalefe, originally weighed a তোলা and ftill continues at that ftandard in Chittagong, where it is on that account called the দশ মাসা dofh maafaa rupee, or a rupee weighing ten maafaas. In other parts of Bengal the ftandard weight of a Sicca rupee is confiderably increafed.

The তোলা (which is generally denominated the *Sicca weight*) is the ftandard unit for the Sar, which varies in almoft every province of India. Thus at Calcutta the Bazar mon is of 80 tolaas i.e. each Sar is to weigh 80 tolaas. The factory mon confifts only of 74 ficca weight or tolaa.s

The fractional parts of the rupee are আনা the aanaa, পাই the paa*ee* or pye, গণ্ডা the gondaa, and কড়ি *cowry*.

The fractions of the কাহন the kaahon, in kaachaa accounts,

are

are প‌ন the pɔn, গণ্ডা the gondaa, and কড়ি the koree.

5 gondaas of a kaachaa account are in the Bazar called one বুড়ি booree, 5 gondaas of a paakaa account conftitute one পাই paaee. Obferve that the word booree is never ufed in accounts, but only in the markets.

20 gondaas make one পোন kaachaa, or one আনা paa‌kaa. The gondaas as far as 19 are marked by the common numerals; after which the fraƈtional mark ⟋. is applied for the pɔns or aanaas. For 2 and 3 pɔns the numerals 2 and 3 are joined to this fraƈtional figure thus ⅄. ℈. and for 4 pɔns, the loweft fraƈtional, or that which fingly denotes the koree, is put before a dot thus |. For 8 pɔns, or aanaas, this fraƈtion is doubled, thus ||. and for 12 pɔns 2 fraƈtional figures con‌neƈted at the top and bottom by a third placed obliquely, thus ഄ. as may be better obferved in the following table.

| 1 koree.
|| 2 korees.
ഄ 3 korees.   4 korees make
১ 1 gondaa.
৫ 5 gondaas one booree kaachaa,   (or one paaee paakaa.)
১০ 10 gondaas kaachaa. (called আধানা aadhaanaa paa‌kaa, half an aanaa.)

১৫ 15 gondaas kaachaa. (or 3 paa*ee* paakaa) 20 gondaas make

/. 1 pon kaachaa, (or·one aanaa paakaa.)

৵. 2 pons.

৶. 3'pons. ৷৹4 pons kaachaa make one চোক chok. (4 pons paakaa make one সিকি *feekee*.)

|. 1 chok or *feekee*, generally denominated 4 pons.

|/. 5 pons kaachaa. (or 5 aanaas paakaa)

|৵. 6 pons.

|৶. 7 pons.

||. 8 pons, or 2 chok (or *feekees*.)

|∣/. 9 pons.

||৵. 10 pons.

||৶. 11 pons.

৸. 12 pons, or 3 choks (or *feekees*.)

৸/. 13 pons.

৸৵. 14 pons.

৸৶. 15 pons. 16 pons kaachaa make 4 *feekees* or 1 kaahon. 16 aanaas paakaa make

১ টাকা 1 taakaa or rupee.

Tables

Tables of Weights and Meaſures.

রতি Rotee.

১১	১২	১৩	১৪	১৫	১৬	১৭
1.	2.	3.	4.	5.	6.	7.

8 Rotees make one যাস maaſaa, which is marked by tranſ‑poſing the fractional ſtroke thus,

যাস Maſaa.

১।	২।	৩।	৪।	৫।	৬।	৭।	৮।	৯।
1.	2.	3.	4.	5.	6.	7.	8.	9.

10 Maaſaas make one তোলা tolaa, which is marked by the common numerals thus,

তোলা Tolaa.

১	২	৩	8
1.	2.	3.	4.

Here begins the table for common weights and meaſures.

As the Tolaa is properly the conſtituent unit of the Sar, and as whatever be the weight of the Sar, that of the Tolaa is always invariable, for the ſake of regularity we will take the Sar of 80 tolaa, of which 5 will make one chotaak.

ছটাক Chotaak.	৴.	৵.	৶.	
	1.	2.	3.	4 Chotaak make one

পোয়া Poaa.	।.	॥.	৸.	
	1.	2.	3.	4 Poaa make one Sar, thus

marked, সের

৴১ ৴২ ৴৩ &c. 40 Sar make ১ মন one Mon.

A Table of Long-meafure.

3 জব barley corns make one আঙ্গুলি or fingers breadth.

4 আঙ্গুলি make one মুঠ or hand.

4 মুঠ make one হাত or cubit.

4 হাত make one ধনুক bow's length or fathom

2000 ধনুক make one ক্রোস kros, or near two

miles and a quarter.

I fhall now give a few inftances of kaachaa and paakaa accounts, which will clearly explain both their arithmetical pofi-
tion, and their mode of numeration.

Account kaachaa.   কড়ি

1. .   .   .   .   ১৷৴৭৷

2. .   .   .   .   ২৷৴৷৷

3. .   .   .   .   ৩৷১০

The numeration of the above fums is as follows:

for the firft line,

এক কাহন ছয় পন সওয়া সাত গণ্ডা 1 kaahon,

for the fecond line,   [6 pons, 7 gondaas and a quarter.

দুইকাহন নয় পন দুই কড়া 2 kaahons, 9 pons, 2 koraas.

for

for the third line,

তিন কাহন সাড়ে চারি পন ₃ kaahons, four pons and a half, or ₁o gondaas.

Account paakaa ভঙ্কা

1.   •   •   •   •   •   •   • ২।২।১০

2.   •   •   •   •   •   •   • ৫ ৴।১০

3.   •   •   •   •   •   •   • ৬৶ ৫

4.   •   •   •   •   •   •   • ৯ ২।৫

5.   •   •   •   •   •   •   • ১৮ ।৷

for the firſt line,

দুই টাকা সাড়ে সাত আনা ₂ rupees, ₇ aanaas, ₁o [gondaas.

for the ſecond line,

পাঁচ টাকা আড়াই আনা ₅ rupees, 2 aanaàs ₁o gondaas.

for the third line,

ছয় টাকা সওয়া তের আনা 6 rupees, ₁₃ aanaas, ₁5 [gondaas.

for the fourth line,

নয় টাকা পৌনে চারি আনা 9 rupees, 4 aanaas, ₁5 [gondaas.

for the fifth line,

এক টাকা পাঁচ আনা এক কড়া ₁ rupee, 5 aanaas, ₁ koree.

It muſt be remembered that the Bengaleſe reckon one paaee

as

as containing 5 gondaas and 4 paa*ees* to the aanaa. Put the Engliſh who generally uſe the paa*ee* as the loweſt denomination in
their accounts, divide the Bengal paa*ee* into three, and reckon
12 paa*ees* to the aanaa, conſequently the Engliſh paa*ee* contains
1 gondaa and two thirds, or ſomewhat more than 6 cowries.

CHAPTER. VII.

OF THE SYNTAX.

TO thoſe who are acquainted with the general rules of grammatical arrangement, the conſtruction of the Bengal idiom
will preſent but few difficulties. While the conſtituent parts of
all languages are the ſame, the modes of combination cannot
be widely different: ſo that to compoſe a new ſyntax, ſome anomalous tongue ſhould be ſought, in which the mutual relation
of the noun, the verb and the particle is neither expreſſed by
inflexion, nor poſition.

But as ignorance, idleneſs and affectation are continually producing a variety of corruptions in every living language, and

X

more

more particularly in Bengal, where there are no native grammarians to check the progrefs of vitious expreffions, or the prevalence of provincial and foreign dialects, it may be thought in
fome degree ufeful to have inveftigated and afcertained the idiom
by fome precife and authoritative ftandard.

A comparative view of the more antient authors, with an
occafional recourfe to the pure Shanfcrit, has furnifhed a clue
for this undertaking; and I am clearly convinced that a due
attention to the examples inferted in the foregoing pages, will
abundantly prove that the Bengal language poffeffes a fund of
words adequate to almoft every branch of compofition; that it
has undergone many material and fucceffive improvements; and
and that its ftyle is capable of regularity, of concifenefs, and of
precifion.

Little indeed can be urged in favour of the bulk of the modern Bengalefe. Their forms of letters, their modes of fpelling,
and their choice of words are all equally erroneous and abfurd.
They can neither decline a word, nor conftruct a fentence: and
their writings are filled with Perfian, Arabic and Hindoftanic
terms, promifcuoufly thrown together without order or meaning: often unintelligible, and always embarraffing and obfcure.

They generally omit the diacritical terminations, or add them

where

where not wanted; drop the perſonal ſigns of verbs, or ſubſtitute one perſon for another; lengthen vowels that ſhould
be ſhort, and curtail thoſe that are properly long. They ſeldom ſeparate the ſeveral words of a ſentence from each other,
or conclude the period with a ſtop. Yet the language with all
theſe corruptions and impediments circulates thro' an extenſive
kingdom, and ſuffices for the mutual intercourſe of ſeveral millions of people. But the want of a better ſyſtem enforces its
practice, and habit gradually reconciles us to its defects.

The Shanſcrit language, among other advantages, has a great
variety in the mode of arrangement: and the words are ſo knit
and compacted together, that every ſentence appears like one
compleat word. When two or more words come together *in
regimine*, the laſt of them only has the termination of a caſe; the
others are known by their poſition; and the whole ſentence ſo
connected forms but one compound word, which is called a
পদ or *foot*.

So in the better Bengaleſe compoſitions the diacri ical terminations are very frequently omitted, and particularly that of
the genitive;   as

কিবা সুনলিত কেশের ভাতি ।
মনিন হইন ননিন পাত ॥

"How

" How beautiful was the jet of her treſſes !

" *The huſband of the lotus* (the beetle) pined away (with envy.)

And when two or more ſubſtantives are put in oppoſition, the diacritical termination of caſe is applied only to the laſt ; as

যুধিষ্ঠির নৃপতিরে ধরিব নিশ্চয়

" I will undoubtedly ſeize the *commander Joodheeſhteer.* "

When two ſubſtantives come together, the genitive is always prior in poſition, unleſs by poetic licence ; as in the following line.

ঝরঝরি জলের বায়ুর থরথরি

" There is *the daſhing of the water*, and the ruſtling of the breeze.

By the ſame liberty the genitive is ſometimes placed at a diſtance from the noun on which it depends ;   as

নক্ষ নক্ষ বীরের কাটিয়া পাড়ে যাতা ।
কাহার কাটয়ে ধনু কার মাথে ছাতা ॥

" Having cut off the heads of thouſands *of heroes*, he throws
[them down ;

" Of ſome he cuts the bows, and of ſome the umbrellas on their
[heads."

There is no other form for the poſſeſſive pronoun, but the genitives of the perſonals ; as আমার *mine*, তোর *thine*, তোমার *your*, তার *his*, আমার দিগের *our* &c.

Example.

Example.

তোমার হাথে রহিন জত আমার ধন

" All my wealth (i.e. the wealth of me) remained in your hands.
" (i.e. the hands of you)

Upon the fame principle the genitive cafe of a fubftantive
may become an adjective; as মধুর *fweet* from মধু *honey.*

Example.

আস্বাষ করিয়া বলে মধুর বচন

" Having infpired him with confidence, he gave him fweet
" counfel. (i.e. *honev'd words,* or *words of honey*)

সিওঁতিতে পদ মাতা রাথিতে২ ।
সিওঁতি হইল সোনা দেথিতে২ ।।
সোনার সিওঁতি দেথি পাটনীর ভয় ।
এত মেয়া মানুষ নয় দেবতা নিশ্চয় ।।

" The mother (of nature) on fuddenly placing her foot in the
[bucket,
" The bucket immediately became gold to behold. "

" Fear feized the pilot, on beholding the *golden* bucket; (and
[he faid)

" This woman is not of human race, fhe is certainly an angel. "

শব্দযোগ or prepofitions, for the moft part govern the
genitive cafe of fubftantives; but frequently the accufative of
pronouns; as

তোমা হইতে নিচ কেবা আছয়ে মানুষে

" Who among men is of lefs account *than yourfelf?*

হে এ রে and আরে are general interjections that mark the vocative cafe; but গো and আন are applied only to women; as

শুন শুন গো সই হিত ঙপদেশ কই রামায়নে কর অবগতি

" Hear, hear, O woman, I give you good advice ; put faith " in the Raamaayon. "

আন পাপিনী আন শঙ্খিনী কেন, নামরিনি হইয়া

" O criminal girl! O forcerefs! wherefore didft thou not " perifh at thy birth ! "

Thefe laft words are alfo ufed unconnectively, to denote that a woman is addreffed by the fpeaker ; as

আন তোর বদন হেরি ৷ সিন্ধু সুতে নিন্দা করি ॥

" O nymph ! when I behold thy cheek, " I defpife the daughter of the ocean "

সীতা গো পরম সতী তার শুন দুর্গতি

" O woman ! Seetaa was very conftant: hear her unfortunate " ftory ! "

রে is alſo uſually ſubjoined to the imperative of the verb, particularly in converſation; as শুনরে *hear* O (thou) for শুন ্বনরে *ſpeak thou*, for বন thus

যাওরে রজনি তুমি মরিয়া

"Gọ thou O night, having periſhed."

The relative is very rarely uſed in compoſition, but its place is conſtantly ſupplied by the perſonal pronoun; as

আছিল রাজার পুত্র কহিল তাহায় ।
পড়িবা সকল পুথি জত লেখা যায় ॥

" There was a Raajaa's ſon, *to him* he ſaid (i.e. to whom he ſaid)
" You ſhall read all the books whatever that are written."

Nouns in the plural number always require a verb in the ſingular; as

সখী গন বলে মহাসয় তুমি কবিবর ।
আমার কি সাধ্য দিতে তোমারে ঊত্তর ॥

" The damſels *ſay*, you, ſir, are a poet.
" What power have we to anſwer you ?

But where reſpect is implied, the plural of the verb is uſed even to a ſingular noun; as

এই রূপে সান্তনা করেন নারায়ন

" In

" In this manner Naaraayon pacifies him. "

And in a refpectful addrefs to fuperiors, the third perfon is generally applied inftead of the fecond ; particularly among the moderns.

The indefinite prefent tenfe of the verb is almoft univerfally applied inftead of the preterite ; and is even put in appofition with it.   Example.

ক্রোধে পার্থ অগ্নিবান পুরিন সন্ধান ।
অগ্নিতে পোড়ায় সৈন্য দ্রোন বিদ্যমান ॥

" Paart,ho in a rage aimed a weapon of fire,
" And with fire *deftroyed* the troops in Dron's prefence. "

The prefent tenfe of the fubftantive verb is always more elegantly underftood, than inferted ;   as

বিদ্যার আকার ধ্যান বিদ্যানাম জপ ।
বিদ্যা লাভ বিদ্যা লাভ বিদ্যা নাম তপ ॥

" The beauty of *Beedyaa is* my ftudy, *Beedyaa's* name *is* my
                                                    [bead-roll ;
" Beedyaa *is* my defire, B*deeyaa is* my defire ; *Beedyaa's* name
is my prayer. "

If a fentence be exprefled conditionally, the expreffion is re-peated in all the words which can admit the conditional form, and the returning member of the period exactly anfwers it ; as

জথন জেমত রাখিবা তথন তেমত পূজিব

" As you fhall at any time place me, *fo* will I *then* worfhip "

The ufe of the conditional conjunction is not confined to the fubjunctive mood ; but is applied to all the tenfes indifferently as in Englifh. Thus:

to the paft,

সোমদত্ত বনে যদি হইনা ক্রপাবান

" Somdott faid, if you *were* really favourable ———"

to the future,

যদি মোরে বর দিবা দেব পশুপতি

" If you *will* grant me a favour, O Lord of life———"

to the prefent,

ব্রহ্মা যদি আপনে আসিয়া করে রন ?
তোমারে ধরিতে সে নারিবে কাদাচন ॥

" If Brohmaa himfelf having defcended *makes* war,

" He fhall by no means avail to take you prifoner. "

The infinitive mood is ufually expreffed by the gerund in

তে as

সভা মধ্যে সোমদত্ত পাইয়া অপমান ?
তপস্যা করিতে বনে করিন পয়ান ॥

Y   " Somdott

" Somdott having received this difgrace in the midft of the
                                                              affembly,
" Retired into the defert *to pray.* "

But the verbal infinitive is very frequently ufed in a paffive
fenfe with the verb য।ওন   Example.

মহা ঘোর যুদ্ধ হয় নাযায় লিখনে

" The battle raged with fo great a noife as cannot be written."
(litterally, as cannot go in writing)

Tranfitive verbs are called সকর্ম্ক in Shanfcrit, intranfi-
tives অকর্ম্ক and thofe are denominated দ্বিকর্ম্ক which
govern two fubjective cafes ;   as

বহৃত বচনে কহিল অর্জুনে

" He addreffed much counfel to Orjoon."

The proper mode of arrangement in Bengalefe is, firft to
name the agent, then the fubject, and laftly the verb :   But
the whole order of a fentence feems generally to be the reverfe
of the Englifh method ;   as

জলেতে পূর্ন হইল সংগ্ঞামের স্হল

" The field of battle was full of water. "

The laft member of a period is almoft always expreffed by
the preterite participle, inftead of the tenfe of a verb ; as

যত দুঃখ দিন তোমায় পাপী দুর্য্যোধন ।
আমারে ক্ষেমহ মাতা না রাখিয়া মন ॥

" Whatever moleftation the wicked Doorjjodhon hath caufed you,
" Forgive me, O mother, not having kept it in mind. " (i.e.
and *do* not *keep* it in mind)

সে দেষে এ সব ভোগ জানহ বিশেষ ।
এ বার করহ ভোগ থাকিয়া এ দেষ ॥

" Know, that in this country all this food is plenty,
" Therefore come now and eat, *having remained* in this country."

মল্লিকা ফুলে মানা অগুরু মাথিয়া ।
নিদাঘে বাতাস দিব কাম জাগাইয়া ॥

" Having anointed with *Ogooroo* (a perfume) my necklace of
[the flower *moleekaa*,
" I will excite a breeze in the ftifling calm, *having awakened*
[defire."

This participle is alfo indeclinable, and agrees with a noun
in any cafe ; or may rather be called a nominative abfolute ; as

ভাট যথে শুনিয়া বিদ্যার সমাচার ।
ওথনিন সুন্দরের সুথ পারাপার ॥

" *Having heard* an account of *Beedyaa* from the mouth of Bhaat,
" The inclinations of *Soondor* boiled vehemently. "

where

where শুনিয়া agrees with সুন্দরের a genitive.

The participle paſſive is very frequently uſed with the tenſes of করন to form a ſimple tranſitive verb; as ক্ষেমা করন to forgive, from ক্ষেমন to forgive; as

এথন ইহার ফল করিবার পারি ৷

ধর্ম্ম অনুরোধে তোমা আজি ক্ষেমা করি ৷৷

" Now I am able to puniſh you for this,

" But for the ſake of religion I this day *forgive* you. "

In all the Indian languages the connection of two ſentences is preſerved, by beginning the ſecond period with the participle preterite of the concluding verb of the firſt.   Example.

আর ধনু ধরি বীর পূরিন সন্ধান ৷

সন্ধান পূরিয়া এড়ে দিব অস্ত্র গন ৷৷

" The hero taking another bow, compleated his aim :

" *Having compleated his aim,* he caſt dreadful weapons. "

This is ſomething like the expreſſion in Ovid :

" Congeriem ſecuit, *ſectamque* in membra redegit. "

The participles দিয়া গিয়া and ſome others are frequently redundant.

Exam-

Example.

দুথের ঘরেতে বন্দি করিয়া অনঙ্গ আনল
ভেজাইয়া দিয়া কোন অভিনাসে বিরহ
বাতাসে জানাইনা জুবতী

" Having enflaved me in the houfe of affliction, and *having fet*
" *to it* the fpark of defire,
" How eagerly did you inflame a young girl with the breath
" of perfidy ! "

This participle preterite muft fometimes be rendered with the
fign of the infinitive in Englifh ;   as

গুন সাগর নাগর রায় নগর দেখিয়া যায়

" The learned Naagor goes *to view* the city. "

Thus we may obferve that the ufe of the participles is very
frequent, and not inelegant, as it throws a degree of variety
into the conftruction, and at the fame time renders the fentence
more round and compact.

Through all the foregoing fheets I have earneftly laboured
to give both a reafon and a proof for every rule which I laid
down, and for every particularity which came in review : This
I hope will exculpate me for the number of infipid inftances
which I have been obliged to infert.   It will not be fuppofed
that

that in the continual hurry of a life of bufinefs I could have much leifure to turn over voluminous compofitions for the meer purpofe of felecting poetical expreffions : I generally took thofe which firft occurred, and for the moft part confined my reading to the Mohaabhaarot, which is reckoned one of the moft claffical writings.

CHAPTER VIII.

OF ORTHOEPY AND VERSIFICATION.

IN the preceding chapters I have laid down no other rules for the utterance or omiffion of the inherent vowel, than fuch as properly depend upon the Shanfcrit, and are applicable to the right pronunciation of verfe, wherein every fingle confonant forms a feparate fyllable. But the popular mode of applying it in ordinary converfation ftill remains to be confidered.

The following canons will I hope be found fufficient for the purpofe.

And firft of words concluding with a confonant whofe inherent vowel is not uttered.

All

All fubftantives that contain only two feparate confonants are monofyllabic in Bengalefe, tho' of two fyllables in Shanfcrit; as মন *the heart,* তপ *prayer,* বীর *a hero,* জন *a perfon:* pronounce mon, top, beer, jon, &c.

The fame method obtains, if the latter confonant be a pho-laa, or double; as দন্ত *a tooth,* পুত্র *a fon,* শব্দ *a word:* read dont, pootr, fhobd.

স্থান the prepofition, and fuch others of the attributive clafs, as are properly fubftantives, come under this rule. So alfo ফের *back,,* দূর *far off,* and আর *moreover* are mono-fyllables.

র the fign of the genitive cafe is always mute; as তার *of him,* তোর *of thee,* মোর *of me,* ঘরের *of a houfe* &c. pronounce taar, tor, mor, ghorar. So গন and দল the figns of the plural number, are alwas yof one fyllable.

কোন kon the interrogative *who?* or *what?* is mono-fyllabic.

Names of numbers which have only two confonants are of one fyllable; as এক ak *one,* তিন teen *three,* পাঁচ paach *five,* ছয় choy *fix,* &c.

Whenever in a word containing more than two feparate confonants,

fonants, the laft letter be a confonant, the included vowel is o-
mitted ;   as আকাষ *Æther*, নন্দন *a fon*, বাতাস *wind*:
pronounce aakaafh, nondon, baataas.

Words containing four feparate confonants (which fhould confequently have three fyllables) are frequently contracted into diffyllables, by dropping the inherent vowel of the third confonant;
as দরশন dorofhon, *appearance* is pronounced dorfhon.

Of words terminating with an open confonant.

All adjectives containing only two fingle confonants, or one
fingle and one double, are diffyllables ;   as বড় *large*, ছোট
fmall, মন্দ *bad*, ভাল *good* &c. pronounce boro, choto, mondo,
bhaalo.

Indeclinable particles of two confonants claffed under the head
of pronouns which terminate in   ন generally have their final
confonant open :   as হেন *that*, তেন *fuch*, কেন *why* &c.
read hano, tano, kano.

The enclytics   ক ko, হ ho and ত to always preferve their
inherent vowel ;   as নাহিক naaheeko for নাহি *not*, এত
ato *this* for এ or এই করহ koroho for কর *do thou* &c.

So alfo the particles of two confonants ending with ত are
diffyllabic ; as কত koto *how many*, তত toto *fo many*, জত
joto

joto howmany foever &c.

The following parts of the verb never drop the inherent vowel of their final confonant:

The 2d. perfon plural of the prefent tenfe; as কর *koro ye do.*

The 3d perfon fingular of the preterite করিল *koreelo he did.*

The 1ft perfon fingular of the future করিব *koreebo I will do.*

The 3d perfon fingular of the aorift করিত *koreeto he would do.*

The 2d perfon fingular and plural of the imperative কর *koro do thou or ye.*

In all other tenfes and perfons of the verb, the concluding confonant is invariably mute; as করিস *ko ees thou doft,* not *koreefo*; করেন *koran they do,* not *korano*; করিলাম *koreelaam I did,* not *ko eelaamo*; করুক *korcok let him do,* not *korcoko*; করন *koron to do,* not *korono*; করিবার *koreebaar in doing,* never *koreebaaro*; fo করিলেক and করিবেক *he hath done, he will do;* are always pronounced *koreelak* and *koreebak.*

The final confonants of the numerals, from eleven to eighteen inclufive, always preferve their inherent vowel; as এগার *agaaro* not *agaar,* আচার *aat,haaro* not *aat,haar* &c.

The other vowels require no rule; they are always uttered as they are written.

Z

When

When the fame word is repeated twice together, the latter is denoted by the figure ২ as the firſt line which is inferted in the fiftieth page would be conſtantly written by the Bengaleſe in this manner.

টন২ করে জন মন্র২ বায়

Many words of popular and general uſe are uſually contracted in Bengal writings, to avoid delay in the hurry of buſineſs.

The contraction is formed by the firſt letter or ſyllable of the word to be contracted, followed by the figure ০ *onoofwor* the conſtant attendant upon theſe occaſions.

I have here inferted the moſt common of them.

A.	কি৹	for	কিসমত	a village or diviſion.
P.		—	কিস্তি	a boat.
B & H.		—	কিস্তিবন্দি	a rent-roll, an agreement to [pay by inſtaliments.
B & H.	চা৹	—	চানান	an invoice.
B & H.		—	চাকর	a ſervant.
A.	জা৹	—	জামিন	a ſurety or ſecurity.
B & H.	জো৹	—	জোড়া	a pair (or ſuit) of any thing.
P.	জি৹	—	জিম্মেয়	in truſt, or, in the charge of.
A.		—	জিনিস	goods.

A.

A.   ন°   for   নগদ   ready money.

A.   তা° — তানুক   a taalook or fmall zemindarry.
(literally, fomething dependent)

A.   — তারিখ   the date or day of the month.

P.   ত° — তরফ   a fide, or towards.

B & H.   দ° — দর   price, or value.

H.   প° — পরগনে   a pergunneh, or large portion
[of land.

B.   পা° — পাইক   a pike, or watchman.

P.   পে° — পেয়াদা   a peaada (a footman, or mef-
[fenger.

P.   বা° — বাবত   on account of, or belonging to.

B.   ম° — মণ্ডল   a mundul, or chief perfon in
[a village.

P.   মা° — মাহে   the moon.

A.   — মারফত   with, or by the hands of.

A.   — মাহামদ   maahaamod.

মে° for the Englifh Mr.

A.   মো° — মোকাম   a place, prefixed to the name of
[any place.

A.   না° — নাগাইদ   ending with (applied to dates
[of time.

A.

A.   সা° — সাকিম an inhabitant.

B.   হা° — হাওয়ানত to the care of.

B.   ই° — ইস্তুক beginning with (applied to dates
[of time.)

NB. A ftands in this lift for Arabic, P for Perfian, H for Hindoftanic, B for Bengalefe.

Of Verfification.

The verfes of the Bengalefe are regulated by accent, and by the number of fyllables in a line ; no regard whatever being paid to quantity, but as it co-incides with accent.

Their poems, like thofe of the Arabians and Perfians, are in Rhyme, which appears to fuit the genius of moft of the Afiatic languages, and to have been in ufe from the earlieft antiquity.

The Bengal Poets have many rules for contracting fuch words as are too long, and for extending thofe that are too fhort for their metre.

The moft common of thefe licences are as follow.

Subftantives are contracted by the omiffion of the diacritical terminations ; of which I have given frequent inftances.

The preterite participle is reduced from three fyllables to two, by changing the penultimate vowel into its correfponding confonant ; as   করা for করিয়া বন্যা for বনিয়া   thus

সাধ করা সিথিনাম কাব্য রস জত ?
কানার কপালে পড়া সব হইল হত ॥

" Having eagerly fought ,   I learnt every fpecies of pleafure ;
" But having fallen to the lot of a deaf man it is all vanifhed. "

The preterites of fome verbs are contracted, by throwing away their penultimate confonant; as কৈনাম for করিনাম I did, বৈনাম I fpoke for বনিনাম Example.

বন মধ্যে বনাৎকার কৈল নারী গন

" In the deferts he committed violence on the women. "

So the firft fyllable of the word পারন to be able, is frequently thrown away, when preceded by the negative না as নারি I am not able, নাপারি নারিনাম for নাপারিনাম &c.

So in the third fingular of the prefent tenfe নহে is not, is contracted to নয় by dropping the হ as

এতেক শুনিয়া সবে বলে হায় হায় ?
যে কথা কহিয়াছ ভাই কিছু মিথ্যা নয় ॥

" Having heard this, they all cried alas, alas !
" The tale which thou haft told, O brother, certainly is not
[falfe. "
Words

Words are lengthened by adding to them ſome one of the following enclytics ক্ৰ *ko* ত *to* হ *ho* and চ *cho.*

The uſage of ক্ৰ *ko* with an open vowel ſeems confined to the word নাহি when it ſtands for *non eſt* ;   as

তোমা সম যোদ্ধাপতি নাহিক আমার

" We have no warrior like yourſelf. "

ত   *to* is applied indifferently wherever a ſyllable is want-ed, but particularly after words ending in ই or এ   as

এই হেত তোমারেত কহি এ রাজন

" On this account I ſpeak to you, O king. "

This enclytic is commonly added after the numerals in com-mon converſation;   as তিনত *teento* for তিন *teen three,* দশত *doſhto* for দশ *doſh ten* &c.

হ *ho* is added to ſome of the pronouns in এ as কেহ *kaho* তেহ *taho* &c. thus

রঘুনাথের বানে তেহ হইল অস্থির

" Even he was put to flight by the arrows of Roghoonaant,h. " and to the ſecond perſons of the preſent tenſe and imperative ;

যদি না করহ মোর বাক্যের পানন

" If

" If you do not furely obey my words,—— "

চ after the Shanfcrit accufative; as নিবেদনঙ্ক for নিবেদন॰ কার্য্যঙ্ক for কার্য্য॰ &c.

The vowel এ is very frequently added enclytically to the cafes of fubftantives.

It is likewife ufed to lengthen out the firft perfon fingular of the prefent tenfe, by inferting after the final ই its correfponding confonant য় as কহিয়ে *I fpeak*, for কহি জানিয়ে *I know*, for জানি Example.

আমি যে কহিয়ে তাহা শুন ক্ষেত্রিগন

" Hear, O ye Kyhatrees, that which I fpeak. "

And alfo to the third perfon of the fame tenfe which ends in এ by changing that vowel into য় as আছিয়ে for আছে করে for কর্য়ে &c. Example.

তোমা হইতে নীচ কেবা আছয়ে মানুষে?
মোর অগোচর নহে জানিয়ে বিশেষে ॥

" Who among men is of lefs account than yourfelf !

" Neither is this hidden from me, I know it well. "

আ is fometimes inferted before এ which is then changed into য় as মাঝায় for মাঝে the locative cafe of মাঝ

the

the middle or *waiſt* ;   as

কে বনে অনঙ্গঅঙ্গ দেখা না যায় ?
দেখুক যে আঁখি ধরি বিদ্যার মাঝায় ॥

" Who ſays that the figure of Love is not to be ſeen ?
" Opening his eyes let him look on the ſhape of *Beedyaa.* "

Of the formation of Verſes.

The Bengal meaſures are altogether borrowed from the Shan-ſcrit, and may be divided into three ſpecies : Heroic, Lyric, and the গীত or Elegiac.

Every line of every ſpecies of verſe is called a ছন্দ with a different additional appellation according to the number of ſyllables it may contain ;   as

অনুষ্টুপ ছন্দ — a verſe of 8 ſyllables.
পংক্তী ছন্দ — — of 10 .
ত্রিষ্টুপ ছন্দ — — of 11 .
জগতী ছন্দ — — of 12 .
শর্করী ছন্দ — — of 14 .

and if the verſe have a double rhyme, which gives it any add number of ſyllables above 11, the word অতি is prefixed to that which denotes the even number immediately below it ;

as

as অতিজগতী a verſe of 13 ſyllables.

অতিশর্করী — of 15 — &c.

The metre moſt uſually applied in Shanſcrit poems is a ſtanza compoſed of four lines, of the অনুষ্টপ ছন্দ each of which
anſwers to a dimetre Iambic, and is called শ্লোক which is a
general term for any ſtanza. The 2d and 4th lines only rhyme
together ; and conſequently make a long diſtich.

বসুনা বসুধা লোকে বন্ধতে মন্ডজাতিকং ৷
করভোরু রতিপুঙ্গে দ্বিতীয়ে পঞ্চমে প্যহং ৷৷

boſoonaa boſoodhaa loka bondota mondo jaateekung
korobhoroo roteepronga dweeteeya ponchoma pyohung.

The common heroic meaſure of the Bengaleſe is a diſtich conſiſting generally of 14 ſyllables, and hath a trochaic accent ; as

দুর্গা দুর্গা পরা তুমি দুর্গতি নাশিনী ৷
গোকুল রাখিলা জয়া যশোদা নন্দিনী ৷৷

doorggaa doorggaa poraa toomee doorggotee naaſheenee
gokoolo raakheelaa joyaa joſhodaa nondeenee.

" O Doorgaa, Doorgaa ! thou art the greateſt of deities and the
[diſpeller of care.

" Thou didſt victoriouſly guard Gokool, thou art the daughter
[of Joſhodaa. "

Aa   This

This ſpecies is called পয়ার Another ſort of diſtich is called তোটকছন্দ and conſiſts of 12 ſyllables with an anapæſtic meaſure.

নৃপনন্দন কাম রসে বসিয়া ।
পরি ধান ধুতি পড়িছে খসিয়া ॥

nreepo nondono kaamo roſa boſeeyaa

poree dhaano dhootee poreech,ha khoſeeyaa.

Sometimes the তোটক has but 11 ſyllables, and then is dactylic with a trochee at the end; as

কি ব্যাধি জন্মিল হিয়ার মাঝে ।
চাঁদের কর শর হেন বাজে ॥

kee byaadhee jonmeelo heeyaaro maajha

chaadaro koro ſoro hano baaja.

" What diſorder is ariſen within my body !
" The rays of the moon pierce me like darts.

All the lyric meaſures of the Bengaleſe (at leaſt ſuch as enter into their larger compoſitions) are alſo diſtichs ; but are ſubdivided by pauſes, and internal rhymes, from whence they receive their appellation.

Thus a line of 14 ſyllables, compoſed of two verſes of 7 ſyllables each, is called এক পদী or *of one pauſe* ;   as

নিজ কর্ম্মের দোষ   তোমারে করি রোষ

" Should I blame you for the criminality of my own actions ? "

A diftich having two paufes in each line of 14 fyllables is
called দ্বিপদী as

পদ্ম সঙ্গে   গাথে রঙ্গে   স্থল পদ্ম ভান ?
মাঝে মাঝে   গন্ধরাজে   আর করে আন ॥

" With joy he ftrings along with the lotus the beautiful ftolo-
[podm ; (a large flower)

" The lilly inferted between them receives additional luftre. "

We have lyric meafures in Englifh which anfwer to all thefe
verfes of the Bengalefe :   Thus in Milton.

" As when the dove, laments her love, all on the naked fpray ;

" When he returns, no more fhe mourns, but loves the live-long
(day. "

But if the diftich have two internal paufes, and confift of more
than 14 fyllables in a line, it is called ত্রিপদী or *of three pau-*
fes ; as in this of 20 fyllables.

পার্থ মহা বীর   হইল অস্থির   পুত্রের মরন শুনি ?
হাহা পুত্র মোর   এক ধনুর্দ্ধর   বীর গন চূড়া মনি ॥

" Part,ho

" Paart,ho the great hero became diſtracted on hearing the
(death of his ſon,

" Alas ! my ſon, the greateſt of all bowmen, the diadem of
all heroes. "

Other treepodees have 7 ſyllables in each of the internal pauſes, and others 8 ; with 10 in the concluding one ; but are all
formed upon the ſame principal.

If there are 3 internal pauſes, rhyming together, beſides the
concluding part, the diſtich is then denominated চৌপদী as

আ গোমরাযাই নইয়াবানাই শলে দিয়াছাই
ভজি ইহারে ৷
যোগিনী হইয়া ওহারে নইয়া যাইপনাইয়া
সাগর পারে ৷৷

" O woman ! I could take upon myſelf his misfortunes, and
" die ; and having conſigned my family to the duſt, would o-
" bey him alone : I would become a pilgrim, and having taken
" him with me, would fly acroſs the ocean. "

The Bengaleſe' fill the pages of their books with verſe as if it
were proſe. The firſt line of a diſtich is diſtinguiſhed by a ſingle upright ſtroke, thus ৷ and the ſecond line by two ſtrokes ৷৷

Muſic

Muſic is conſtantly applied by the Hindoos in all their public worſhip ; but the inſtruments on which it is performed are
very imperfect, and ſeem hardly to have received any alterations, or improvements from the firſt period of their invention.
The Bengaleſe always uſe the minor key, and their gamut proceeds by the very ſmalleſt intervals of the chromatic ſcale. They
have no idea of counterpoint, and always play and ſing in uni-
ſon or octaves.

Their ſyſtem is divided into ſix modes called রাগ each of
which is ſuppoſed to be adapted to particular ſeaſons and circumſtances according as its peculiar character is grave or gay, loud or
ſoft &c. Every রাগ is ſubdivided into ſix ſubordiante modes
denominated রাগিনী and it is to be obſerved that as রাগ is
of the maſculine gender, and রাগিনী of the feminine, the
Hindoos ſuppoſe রাগ to be the huſband, and রাগিনী his
wives. I have been told that there are treatiſes in Bengaleſe
and Shanſcrit upon the ſcience of muſic, but I could never procure a ſight of them. The book called রাগমালা (or *the
necklace of muſic*) is nothing more than a collection of pictures,
exhibiting the traditional hiſtory of the primary and ſubordinate
modes, and the ſubjects appropriated to each.

Almoſt

Almoſt all the Bengal compoſitions are intended to be ſung to the accompaniment of inſtruments, and every change of metre or of ſtrain is regularly marked as it occurs; that no part may be introduced out of ſeaſon, and that a রাগ proper for the morning may not unfortunately be performed in the evening.

In moſt of the poetical writings upon religious or moral ſubjects, which are ſuppoſed to be recited or ſung by a Bramin to a ſurrounding audience, a ſort of hemiſtich or diſtich is occaſionally inſerted to be ſung in chorus by the whole aſſembly at particular intervals. It is not always a verſe belonging to the reſt of the meaſure, but has a ſeparate and diſtinct metre of its own : it is called ধুয়া . When it is to be attended with clapping of hands, as in the ceremonies of public worſhip, ধুয়া তান

In all the larger works, various kinds of metre are applied to enliven the ſtyle, or to expreſs particular change of ſentiments and paſſions : ſo in the Dron porb of the Mohaabhaarot where the lamentation of Orjjoon for the death of his ſon is introduced, the narrative of the accident is in the পয়ার or common heroic; but when Orjjoon himſelf begins to ſpeak, the meaſure ſuddenly breaks

breaks off into the ত্রিপদী beginning পার্থ মহা বীর হইন অস্থির &c.

The গীত or elegiac ſtyle of writing, is ſo very looſe and arbitrary, that I cannot lay down any rules for its conſtruction; but I have generally obſerved, that the ſame rhyme is carried on thro' the whole ode.

The ſtrain of theſe pieces ſeems in general to be much more poetical than that of their more extenſive compoſitions.

APPENDIX.

Hitherto we have ſeen the formation and conſtruction of the Bengal language in all its genuine ſimplicity ; when it could borrow Shanſcrit terms for every circumſtance without the danger of becoming un-intelligible, and when tyranny had not yet attempted to impoſe its fetters even on the freedom of compoſition.

As a contraſt to this, I ſhall take for the ſubject of this appendix a ſhort petition which I have ſelected from a number of others as being remarkably replete with foreign expreſſions ; and which ſerves to ſhew how far the modern Bengaleſe have been

forced

forced to debafe the purity of their native dialect, by the neceffity of addreffing themfelves to their Mahommedan Rulers. Indeed the Muffulman officers, who fuperintended the adminiftration of juftice and the collection of the revenues, would feldom or never condefcend to receive petitions and letters in the Bengal language, with which they were almoft wholly unacquainted: but obliged the natives to procure a Perfian tranflation to all the papers which they might have occafion to prefent. This practice familiarifed to their ears fuch of the Perfian terms as more immediately concerned their feveral affairs; and by long habit, they learnt to affimilate them to their own language, by applying the Bengal inflexions and terminations.

I fhall firft infert the petition as it ftands in the original, copied exactly on a copper plate, and reprefented in the proper character on the correfponding page. This will fhew the learner moft of the vitiated forms of letters ufed in expeditious writing; and introduce him to the irregular hands, which are conftantly found in matters of bufinefs.

I fhall next give a plain, but not literal tranflation of the petition, meerly to fhew its meaning, and laftly fhall analyze the conftruction of each word, and point out its derivation.

৭বৰম

গাইবানাবাবেসেনমত

আনাবনাইদাইণবাসানবেন

জাবেবইয়ামাবীযাশীকিশণীববযাাে

সেইবইয়ামাসত্রী হয়াাহোকানবববপুেব

বহাবঙ্খতেঈ্রবিআপবাবতযবদ্তী দমেনসবীযা

ভোকাবীতে আমীমানসকাইবসাবযাাৢে

মাবাগাতেই ৩মেব্যাবতেশববাযেবিতআধী

ববতোণদাববববাযীবক পশুচিযা তেবেলাবে

নেবাদিযাাবযাতআদানত সবযাবুদাবেবসানাযা

সেবাৈ সমাসত সালাইবয— ১১ কাৰ

CW Sculpt.⹀

For EU product safety concerns, contact us at Calle de José Abascal, 56–1°,
28003 Madrid, Spain or eugpsr@cambridge.org.

www.ingramcontent.com/pod-product-compliance
Ingram Content Group UK Ltd.
Pitfield, Milton Keynes, MK11 3LW, UK
UKHW010338140625
459647UK00010B/684